Baudrillard and Theology

Baudrillard and Theology

James Walters

t & t clark

Published by T&T Clark International
A Continuum Imprint

The Tower Building   80 Maiden Lane
11 York Road   Suite 704
London   New York
SE1 7NX   NY 10038

www.continuumbooks.com

Excerpts from *Symbolic Exchange and Death* by Jean Baudrillard reproduced by permission of SAGE Publications Ltd., London, Los Angeles, New Delhi, Singapore and Washington DC (Sage, 1993).

British Library Cataloguing-in-Publication Data
A catalogue record for this book is available from the British Library.

ISBN: HB: 978-0-5675-4395-0
PB: 978-0-5675-5972-2

Typeset by Deanta Global Publishing Services, Chennai, India
Printed in India

CONTENTS

Acknowledgements viii

Introduction: Overcoming the real 1

PART ONE 9

1 Signs, systems and '68 11
    Baudrillard's context: Philosophical 11
    Baudrillard's context: Political and economic 18
    Moving on from Marx 21

2 Simulation and the hyperreal 26
    The order of simulacra 27
    The metaphysics of the code 32
    The implosion of religion 36

3 Exchange: Economic and symbolic 41
    Fatality and totality 41
    Symbolic exchange 46
    Seduction 51

4 Life after God 55
    Impossible exchange 56
    The age of the non-event 58
    Alterity in a whitewashed life 61

PART TWO 65

5 Sacraments and simulacra 67
   Sign and symbol 69
   The ceremony of the world 73
   Sacramental singularities 77

6 Eschatology, terrorism and death 80
   The illusion of the end 81
   Taking charge of death 84
   Realized eschatology: Singularity and *kairòs* 91

7 Beyond good and evil 94
   The relentless positivity of the global 95
   Globalization and the good 101

8 Barred bodies 106
   Body as sacred consumer object 107
   The barred body 109
   From sexual difference to transsexuality 111
   Sacramental body 115

9 Fragments in the desert 119
   The desert of the real 120
   Fragments 123
   Poetic resolution 128

10 Radical otherness 132
   Radical thought 133
   From self to other 136

God of nothing 139
Theological hyperreality 141

Notes 145
Bibliography 170
  Works by Baudrillard 170
  Other works 171
Index 177

ACKNOWLEDGEMENTS

I would like to thank Thomas Kraft and Robin Baird-Smith at Continuum for commissioning this book. I am also grateful to colleagues at Hampstead Parish Church and the London School of Economics for encouragement and support during its writing. Many conversations have shaped my exploration of Baudrillard's ideas, but I am especially grateful to Jamie Hawkey, Peter Selby and John Hughes for discussion of specific chapters, and Greg Seach's attentive reading of the whole work has been totally invaluable. Above all, I must pay tribute to the late Dan Hardy who supervised the doctoral thesis in which I first engaged with the work of Jean Baudrillard. Dan steered me through the potentially overwhelming complexities and enabled me to interpret Baudrillard's unusual post-structuralist writings from an imaginative theological perspective. This book is dedicated to his memory and that of my late grandmother who, while taking no interest in French philosophy, taught me far more about symbolic exchange than any book possibly could. Finally I would like to thank Xavier, Jacqueline and the late Maurice Domino for cultivating my interest in all thing French and for their hospitality on tenuously justified research trips.

Introduction:
Overcoming the real

You can't ask someone who has himself become an icon for a solution to the problem of the image.[1]

What relevance might the work of Jean Baudrillard hold for theology? Or perhaps we should begin with the question of Baudrillard's relevance for any academic discipline. Emerging from the French philosophical tradition, he is given scant attention by academic philosophers. Considered by some as a sociologist (at least in his early work), that is a discipline he himself rejects. He is commonly found in the cultural studies' section of a bookshop, and yet this discipline merely considers narrow aspects of his work. So we may be perplexed by the importance attached to a writer who remains something of an academic nomad or downright misfit. Yet the French economist Marc Guillaume suggests that it is precisely in this peripheral relation to the Academy that Baudrillard's significance lies: 'The little consideration shown for his work by academic authorities can only be seen as reasonable and mostly positive. We should not try to compensate for this fortunate oversight but be the guardians of the freedom that this work introduces into thought by saving it from restrictive reductions'.[2] Baudrillard is a free thinker, unconstrained by standard methodologies or systems of thought, and that, if nothing else, ought to appeal to the theologian.

At its heart, Baudrillard's work is concerned with a radical reappraisal of our perception of the Real in the contemporary world. His work is intensely observational, not from any neutral, dislocated perspective, but immersed in the distortions and simulations he describes. Baudrillard is not just an academic nomad but a literal nomad of the Western consumer society. In his 1986 work, *America*, he writes, 'Where others spend their time in libraries, I spend mine in the deserts and on the roads. Where they draw their material from the history of ideas, I draw mine from what is happening now, from the life of the streets or the beauty of nature'.[3] Baudrillard's exploration of what is real – or has been lost into what he describes as the Hyperreal – arises out of attentiveness, a kind of deep phenomenology that looks beyond the commonly accepted pattern and presentation of events to see more complex realities at work. Baudrillard looks through the banality of the immediately visible to identify invisible forces. As such he is not afraid to identify his own approach with that of the mystic, resisting a conventional ordering of events to look more deeply into their significance. Asked in an interview in 1995 about his reading of history, he replied, 'I do not have an historical perception of events. But I would say that I have a mystical reading of them and that history for me would be a long narrative which I tend to mythologise'.[4]

So when we recognize that Baudrillard has more in common with the mystic than with the philosopher, we begin to see that he may indeed have some relevance to theology. He has also commented that he is less a sociologist than 'a metaphysician, perhaps a moralist'.[5] But it must be acknowledged that this is certainly an unconventional kind of mysticism or metaphysics. He shows little interest in the concept of 'God' as a primary agent in the world, following Nietzsche as he develops the notion of the 'death of God'. One of the few things he says about himself in his writings includes 'I am a nihilist'.[6] Traditionally conceived transcendental explanations of the material world hold no weight for Baudrillard. He certainly employs concepts, anecdotes and terminology from the Christian tradition as part of the bricolage of metaphors he uses to elucidate meaning. Yet he does not treat the theological thought that he has encountered with a high degree of seriousness.

But this is not to say that his meditations on reality's multiple layers could not offer much to the development of theology today. As theology considers its present predicament of some marginalization, it cannot simply retreat into a self-referential world of its own exhausted terminology, a language which, as Paul Janz has argued, 'has today become remote, anachronistic and meaningless with regard to its truth or reality in life'.[7] Too much theological discourse now seeks to justify itself on its own terms, with little regard for the meaningfulness of its concepts to ordinary life. Indeed some forms of post-liberal theology almost wear this disconnection as a badge of honour. But it is no denigration of revelation to reconsider how the Christian narrative translates into the lived experience of the world around us, as we experience it today. It is from the logic of the Incarnation that Janz argues 'theology must even today always look nowhere else but to the world of sensible-rational human embodiment, in and for which the reality of God is disclosed, and never away from this world'.[8] So this must require something of Baudrillard's style of acute attentiveness to and immersion in the world around us as the strategy theologians must employ. Attending to the world and the 'signs of the times' is not the opposite of attending to God.

What Baudrillard's work adds to this is the perspective that the very process of looking at the world attentively reveals that what we might have considered 'sensible and rational' is, in the present age, less obviously so. What was once real and observable in concrete terms is now less readily examined, suggesting that it is not merely theology that is facing a crisis of meaning and coherence today. Baudrillard contends that, 'right now, the sciences are incapable of according a definite status to their object'.[9] The sociologist Richard Sennett identifies our basic cultural problem as the fact that 'much of modern social reality is illegible to the people trying to make sense of it'.[10] The financial crisis of 2008 (the year after Baudrillard died) has revealed that this profound illegibility extends to the primary processes of the capitalist system which have so shaped our patterns of life and thought through the twentieth century. Through this period, our openness to the transcendent receded in the face of a scientific rationalism that seemed to be embodied by the unstoppable logic of market exchange, a force that continues to reshape our world in this era of globalization. Yet now the unquestioned 'realism' of these economic structures has been exposed; they are their own mythology. As Robert Skidelsky has argued, 'The economists' definition of rational behaviour as behaviour consistent with their own models, with all other behaviour dubbed as irrational, amounts to a huge project to reshape humanity into people who behave the way economists say they should behave'.[11]

For some decades, Baudrillard has been calling us to an awakening to the dangers of these kinds of constructions. He argues that, through the processes that construct and distort our day-to-day experience, what we once believed to be intensively present to us is now extensively dissipated, even our own subjectivity. It is clear that such radical arguments are not easily heard within everyday public discourse or academic debate. So his writing is designed to unsettle and disturb as much as to convince and explain. He frequently sets light to detailed argument and shocking generalized assertions will be left unsubstantiated. Indeed, so keen is he to provoke that rhetoric often supersedes coherent argument. As Douglas Kellner bemoans, 'Contradictions do not bother Baudrillard, for indeed he affirms them. It is thus tricky to argue with Baudrillard on strictly philosophical grounds and one needs to grasp his mode of writing, his notion of theory fictions, and to engage their saliency and effects'.[12] Little surprise, therefore, that many find his condemnatory commentary on life unconvincing and dismiss him as too hyperbolic and self-aggrandized. Nicholas Zurbrugg speaks for much of the scholarly establishment in his witty judgement that:

> Baudrillard's barbs wing their way not so much from the heights of visionary hyperspace as from the revisionary realm of fin-de-siècle sniper-space, reflecting on and deflecting away from their subject matter as factual or semi-factual observation transmutes into oneiric overstatement. In this respect, Baudrillard's self-indulgent 'fictions' charm and disarm both their reader and their writer as one senses one's critical sensibility gradually disintegrating and evaporating in the wake of his beguiling generalizations.[13]

There is indeed something beguiling about Baudrillard. He has become, as his words quoted at the opening of this introduction suggest, his own iconic brand. This grew dramatically after the reference to his work in the hit film *The Matrix*,[14] a link based, in his own words, on 'a misunderstanding' of his work.[15] His ambivalent depictions of the postmodern condition can easily be corralled into endorsements or condemnations of 'the way we live now' by radical and conservative alike. In my view, what is most dangerous for the theologian in reading Baudrillard is that, for all its observational character, there is also a sense in which sometimes his deliberations, as Zurbrugg notes, 'overlook the actuality of contemporary culture'.[16] Much of his work irritates people because he paints a picture of what life does or does not mean for others while paying scant attention to how they might experience or narrate it themselves.

As a significant example of this, Baudrillard caused indignation in the United States after the 9/11 terrorist attacks for saying that 'the horror for the 4,000 victims of dying in those towers was inseparable from the horror of living in them – the horror of living and working in sarcophagi of concrete and steel'.[17] Characteristically, he read the atrocity purely as 'a major symbolic event', making no reference to the depth of personal tragedy involved and the quality of human relationship (even in this iconic centre of capitalism) witnessed, for example, in telephone messages left for loved ones on that day. The reason for this is the dominance of the structuralist philosophical tradition in his thought over the existentialist/phenomenological approach (explored in the first chapter).[18] One can certainly defend his right to a purely symbolic reading, not least because of the way in which the more popular, emotive readings have been used as the justification of much subsequent violence. Indeed we might praise his courage in placing 9/11 in the context of the unseen violence of today's global capitalism. Nonetheless, the theologian must surely combine any dispassionate, structural reading with one that attends more deeply to the gift and sanctity of the human lives involved, one that asks, 'what is God doing in this person's life? What violence is being done to her and what is the vision of society that will cause her to flourish with and for others?'

It is with these cautions and caveats in place that I wish to pursue Baudrillard's usefulness to contemporary theology. And I hope that this book will demonstrate what I believe to be the considerable scope of that usefulness since, while he appears to pay insufficient attention to human experience, my contention is that a concern for deep human interconnectedness is what drives Baudrillard's work. He seeks the symbolic relation between people that market exchange has eroded and his bleak description of what has replaced it is a provocation to rediscover it. This crisis of human sociality (cognitive, political, ecological) that Baudrillard recounts must be the primary concern of theology today. In this book, I hope to set out how Baudrillard's work might provide resources for the reconception of theological meaning beyond the idealist categories of the past to recover an understanding of God's redemptive work in creation today.

It must be stated that what I am not attempting in this book is a systematic refutation of Baudrillard's atheistic and nihilistic thought from a theological standpoint. Others engage in that kind of enterprise, but I am more concerned to see what possibilities his rampant hermeneutics of suspicion might open up for the theologian. I use his deconstructionist ideas as a springboard for contemporary theology. The book is therefore divided into two parts. Part I seeks to set out the essentials of Baudrillard's thought for those unfamiliar with his work. This is by no means an exhaustive survey of his prolific output nor an (essentially futile) attempt to systematize his thought. Rather it is an introduction to his key ideas and the points at which they might connect with theology. It begins by placing him in some context, both the philosophical milieu of late twentieth century France and the political and economic transitions taking place at this time. Chapter 2 then looks at Baudrillard's most celebrated theme of simulation and key ideas of the 'metaphysics of the Code' and our present condition of the hyperreal. This chapter closes with a look at what Baudrillard believes to be the 'imploded' state of religion today. Chapter 3 addresses the fundamental theme of exchange, the modes of interaction between human beings and how Baudrillard believes them to have been corrupted by the generalized logic of market exchange. This has replaced symbolic exchange, a deeper concept of sociality which Baudrillard takes from the work of Marcel Mauss. Chapter 4 draws together some themes of theological interest in his work under the heading 'Life after God'.

Part II consists of six essays drawing out the theological implications of different areas of Baudrillard's work. Those with a predominately theological interest may choose to go directly to these essays without an exhaustive reading of Part I. Chapter 5 takes up Baudrillard's central theme of symbolic exchange and considers this in the context of liturgy and worship. Chapter 6 addresses questions of time and eschatology. Chapter 7 looks at Baudrillard's use of the categories of Good and Evil as a way into some reflection on human flourishing and development. Chapter 8 considers the human body and its centrality as the site of commodification and simulation in the consumer society. Chapter 9 looks at Baudrillard's writing style in the form of the fragment and the poetic, reflecting on how these might inform theological writing. Finally, Chapter 10 considers the core theological questions of engaging with alterity in

Baudrillard's work. It is here that I argue that his nihilism may offer more theological potential than first appears.

As Chapter 9 explains, Baudrillard's mode of writing is as important as its content. There is a real sense with Baudrillard that we are engaging more with texts than with concepts. Consequently I use a significant amount of citation of his work to allow the reader the opportunity to be adequately immersed in his world. I have sought to explain his meaning as much as possible by opening up his unusual lexicon, through reference to other thinkers and through illustrative examples. But just as Baudrillard's philosophy is a critique of philosophy so it is a critique of our desire to understand exhaustively. His writings need to be mused over rather than received or rejected as propositions. Some, in my experience, lead nowhere. But others may serve as prisms through which we begin to see things differently. Such is the risk of radical thought. And for taking those risks, even theology may owe Jean Baudrillard a debt of gratitude.

PART ONE

1

Signs, systems and '68

Even signs must burn.[1]

Baudrillard's philosophical project originates in a systemic analysis of the powerful processes of consumer capitalism, showing how these processes distort the meaning and coherence on which the human self and human relationship depend. Over the half century that he writes, until his death in 2007, his work ranges widely and develops a very idiosyncratic style of both reasoning and writing. But his approach is grounded in this essential project which, while distinctive, also reflects the dominant philosophical and political currents of his day. A particular approach to language, visual culture and revolutionary politics shape his thinking through the 1960s and 1970s in ways that endure throughout his writing, even as it subsequently evolves in unconventional ways. This chapter seeks to place Baudrillard in the philosophical and political context of his time and trace his early break with traditional Marxism after the student riots of 1968.

Baudrillard's context: Philosophical

The philosophical movements that dominated French thought in the second half of the twentieth century can be loosely grouped into two strands: those that begin from the standpoint of the thinking subject (existentialism and phenomenology) and those that emphasize the primacy of the objective systems within which humans operate (structuralism and situationalism). Baudrillard would more naturally be seen as belonging to the latter category and bears many of the features of 'post-structuralism', although he is a difficult thinker to categorize. His thinking is, in some ways, unique and he is consequently omitted from a great number of surveys of French thought of the period.[2] While his early analysis is certainly systemic, he is in fact influenced greatly by both existentialism in the form of Sartre (particularly his development of the Marxist concept of alienation within ordinary social relations)[3] and also Husserl's phenomenological approach of critiquing the character of everyday life and the objects that shape it.

Language

Nonetheless, it is fair to say that Baudrillard's understanding of the world emerges out of the systemic approach known as structuralism that originated in the linguistic analysis of Ferdinand Saussure (1857–1913). The *Cours de linguistic général* was not written by Saussure, but based on notes taken by students from the lectures he gave at the University of Geneva in the early years of the twentieth century. It sets out the most comprehensive exploration ever attempted of what language is and how it works, which has become the basis of a far wider analysis of human systems of meaning. Saussure draws a distinction between language as a series of speech acts (*parole*) which make up the day-to-day processes of communication and language as the system of rules that govern speech (*langue*). This is the system that shapes and determines any given speech act. The language system is made up of signs. But, crucially for Saussure, these signs are not merely referents that point us towards non-verbal concepts (e.g. the sign 'bicycle' might simply be seen as referring to the concept of the two-wheeled pedal vehicle). Saussure rejects the view that language is simply a communication tool that refers us to some other more concrete realm of meaning. For Saussure, ideas and meaning are more closely bound up in the *processes* of language. Indeed, there are no ideas independent from language; ideas may only be understood in relation to language.[4]

Consequently, the Saussurean sign encompasses both word and idea. He understands a sign to be constituted of both a signifier (*signifiant*) and what is signified (*signifié*). Only taken together can they give meaning to the sign. With such an understanding of the sign as the basis of language, Saussure then goes on to elaborate how we should not view signs as meaningful in isolation (as if the word 'bicycle' contained all its meaning within this single signifier), but as part of a system of signs in which individual signs only find their meaning in relation to one another. The sign only communicates within the context of the overall system of signs. More specifically, Saussure contended that the meaning of the sign derives from its *difference* from other signs. Meaning is not found in the content of the linguistic sign, but in its structural relation within the system of differences.

What may seem to be a rather technical debate about the operation of language has in fact had profound impact on wide areas of philosophy. Indeed, Saussure came to view semiology as a general science of signs in which linguistics would be merely one branch. We shall come to see how these ideas underpin Baudrillard's social critique. Saussure articulates the idea of human society's dependency on a system of signs to generate meaning and coherence and Baudrillard takes the notion of the semiotic system and writes it large onto the consumer society that dominates our modes of exchange today. Yet others begin this approach and influence his own work in taking the structuralist method into the anthropological, psychological and social realms of human experience.

Anthropology

Foremost among these is Claude Lévi-Strauss who worked primarily in the area of anthropology. Lévi-Strauss used the Saussurean semiological approach to understand how the signifiers of primitive societies (their customs, rituals and art) relate to those societies' beliefs about kinship relations, gods, purity and pollution and so on (signifieds). Lévi-Strauss rejected a typical functionalist view of these primitive practices as seeking to explain some mystery in the pre-scientific age or perpetuating the authority of a ruling elite. Just as Saussure rejected an instrumentalist view of language, Lévi-Strauss did not regard the ritual language of primitive societies as articulating pre-existing beliefs. Rather he sees the whole ritual system as a sign system through which the community generates meaning. 'He does not see a society or culture as having certain ideas about kinship (or the gods, or animal totems) that are then implemented by practices corresponding to them, the practices being material images of the society's "self-understanding". Rather, both the ideas and the practices are specified by their shared formal structure, once again understood in terms of differences between elements in the system'.[5]

Mike Gane suggests that the televised conversations on art between Claude Lévi-Strauss and Georges Charbonnier in 1959 had a strong impact on Baudrillard.[6] In these dialogues, Lévi-Strauss explored how the art of primitive societies functioned as the sign system of the social group and how the move towards representational art in the Western tradition leads to the diminution of this role. His comparison of primitive and modern societies has a dual significance in its influence on Baudrillard. First, he elaborates strong contrasts between them. He compares the small-scale primitive 'cold' society to a clock, a system which minimizes disorder and entropy and tends towards stability. Modern civilized societies he compares to the steam engine. These 'hot' societies are prone to rapid change, disorder and entropy which require strong social hierarchy to control. In drawing these distinctions, Lévi-Strauss may be guilty of a sentimentalizing of primitive societies (a trait Baudrillard takes even further), but it should, second, be noted that in reading societies in this way he is also rejecting a normative distinction between them. Implicit is a very radical rejection of certain notions of human progress and our ability to talk about early societies as 'primitive' and modern societies as 'advanced'. Unconscious sign systems continue to pervade our culture and he suggests that uncovering these hidden structures of social life remains the primary means of studying human thought and society. This is of enormous significance to Baudrillard who frequently blurs the lines between historical anthropology and contemporary sociology in his writing.

In this anthropological strand, Gane sees a strong Durkheimian paradigm in Baudrillard's work, influenced by the work of Georges Bataille and Marcel Mauss (whose influence will be explored in later chapters). What makes Baudrillard's work frequently strange and unconventional is his strategy of casting himself as the 'primitive' and lauding a seemingly barbaric, ritual society over the supposed rational consumer society of the present day. To Gane, this is Baudrillard's 'remarkable project', to place himself as 'a pre- or anti-rationalist, and to evolve a poetic theoretical analysis of the effects of the most advanced technical transformations in our culture'.[7]

Psychology

Another field in which Saussure's theories were advanced and whose influence can be strongly identified in Baudrillard's work is that of psychology. In the 1960s, structuralist thinkers in this area such as Jacques Lacan began to engage in semiological readings of Freud, reappraising the significance of the Unconscious after its rejection by the existentialists in their emphasis on conscious agency. Lacan suggested that the Unconscious could also be understood as a sign system, a kind of regulative language, made up of the drives and desires that shape conscious behaviour. Lacan labels this realm *the Symbolic*. He conceived of speech and action as the signified of the unconscious signifier, and, again, the meaning of any particular sign can only be discerned within the system of differences. Baudrillard states that his understanding of the Symbolic differs from Lacan's 'Imaginary', giving it a particularly anti-capitalist slant.[8] Nonetheless, he explores the power of the unconscious drives, and particularly the Death Drive, in *Symbolic Exchange and Death* and the notion of the Symbolic as a suppressed but overriding social agent remains a central theme of his work.

But the broader relevance to Baudrillard of this structuralist Freudian approach is perhaps found in its concern with the relation of the individual to broader reality. The very purpose of psychoanalysis in the Freudian tradition is to allow the ego sufficient control over the unconscious that it can relate to reality in a stable way. But Baudrillard comes to the point of suggesting that the complexity and potency of the sign system has now made reality entirely ungraspable. This notion seems already present in Lacan's definition of *the Real* as the perpetually elusive limit of language. For Lacan, psychoanalysis must serve to destroy the illusions of stability in the ego and the objective reality that the ego perceives, subordinating both to the realm of the Symbolic. Here he would seem to prefigure a central theme that Baudrillard would develop – that of death of the human subject in the age of the Hyperreal.

However, of the Freudian structuralists, it is perhaps Julia Kristeva whose work had the greatest impact on Baudrillard in her developing of the two modes of language: semiotic and symbolic.[9] In her analysis of literature, Kristeva suggests that the former is the rule-governed system of language that occurs within the finite field. This interacts with what she calls the dialogical or symbolic, a kind of language involving the 'transfinite' and drawing heavily on unconscious drives and the chaotic world of bodily functions. In psychological terms the semiotic is the realm in which the self is generated but is also the source of its destabilization. The symbolic is the source of the social in which the individual finds stability. In her literary analysis, Kristeva sees ambivalence in language as arising from the confluence of these two modes, an insight which influences Baudrillard's own notion of ambivalence. Kristeva's understanding of the transfinite and symbolic in poetry may lie behind his embracing of this style in his later work, a theme explored in Chapter 9.

Social critique

While his incorporation of these anthropological and psychological perspectives makes his work distinctive, it is, however, his application of the structuralist semiotic approach to the social critique of the Left that dominates Baudrillard's early work. Two other thinkers have a decisive influence on this approach, both of whom he met in the early 1960s while doing editorial work for the French publishing house *Seuil*. The first of these is Roland Barthes who led the way in using the Saussurean semiological method to reconceive the traditional Marxist themes of alienation and class struggle. Barthes developed a distinctive understanding of the way in which signs signified, not simply in isolation, but within the system of signs, to perpetuate political ideology. This he called 'myth' and, in his 1957 work, *Mythologies,* he shows how everyday objects are drawn into the normalization (or naturalization) of unquestioned political ideas. A key example is the signification of clothes within the fashion system, an area which Baudrillard also explores in his early work. But it is not merely clothes that signified in this mythological way. Barthes contended that 'Everything in everyday life is dependent on the representations which the bourgeoisie *has and makes us have* of the relations between man and the world . . . bourgeois norms are experienced as the evident laws of a natural order'.[10] Another example he cites is the way in which the traditional opulent wedding functions as a major class ritual which is held up as an ideal to all sections of society. The mythology of this kind of wedding, however, perpetuates the traditions of the ruling elite and provokes decadent commercial expenditure. Barthes' approach is reflected in both Baudrillard's Marxist analysis of the system of consumer products in *The System of Objects* (1968) and the sociology of consumerism in *The Consumer Society* (1970).

Similar work was carried out by the second influence on Baudrillard in this area: Henri Lefebvre. Closer to the humanism of the Frankfurt School than the rigid structural Marxism of Louis Althusser, Lefebvre did much to popularize Marx's early writing, the central theme of which he saw as the liberation of the human self. For Lefebvre, the key issue was that of alienation. 'Today we are only just beginning to glimpse the complexity of the questions the theory of alienation poses', he argued in his Preface to the Second Edition of the *Critique of Everyday Life*.[11] We must look beyond the macro-economic questions of capital and labour towards the substance (and objects) of the mundane, since 'it is in everyday life that the sum total of relations which make the human – and every human being – a whole takes its shape and its form. In it are expressed and fulfilled those relations which bring into play the totality of the real, albeit in a certain manner which is always partial and incomplete: friendship, comradeship, love, the need to communicate, play, etc'.[12] Thus we see a precedent for Baudrillard's shift in repositioning the traditional questions of political economy in the ordinary world around us, a world that may be read structurally in the semiological mode, but in which we must acknowledge our own sense of immersion and complicity.

The French thinkers discussed above constituted Baudrillard's immediate intellectual environment. Their preoccupation with Marxism contributed to the underlying influence of Hegel whose dialectical suppositions are in the background of Baudrillard's work. Baudrillard's grand narrative of the 'precession of simulacra' that we will explore in the next chapter is reminiscent of the strong forces Hegel believed to be driving each historical epoch. But Baudrillard also styles himself against Hegel in his recurrent position of the impossibility of a dialectic with otherness. The German influences on Baudrillard went beyond Hegel. Through his early translation work, he was more familiar than many of his contemporaries with Schopenhauer, Heidegger and Nietzsche (whose influence on Baudrillard is profound and will be discussed in the subsequent chapters). Richard Lane has also highlighted the impact of the German playwright Peter Weiss (1916–82), four of whose works Baudrillard translated in the 1960s. Lane suggests that Weiss' play Marat/Sade offered 'a new and interesting form for the exploration of political ideas, one which strays far from the typical Marxism'[13] and is mirrored in Baudrillard's engagement with the work of Georges Bataille. This reflects an unusually eclectic range of influences, particularly from avant garde and surrealist thinkers,[14] who lead Baudrillard to cross disciplines and push the boundaries of conventional philosophy in several directions.

Baudrillard's context: Political and economic

The fusion of Marxist thought with Saussurean semiology that we have explored points to significant transitions taking place in the capitalist economy at this time. Much of Baudrillard's own work might be seen as a response to these transitions. The 1968 riots, fermented by many of Baudrillard's students at Nanterre, failed to bring about the kind of systemic change for which many radicals had hoped and prompted an intractable crisis for Marxist intellectuals. This violent expression of disaffection with static social structures and injustice seemed to many to be full of the promise of a new world order. In reality the riots, confined largely to the universities, resulted in little more than reform of their own institutions. So the events of May 1968 hastened a creative reinvention of Marxism (including the work of Lefebvre, Barthes and Baudrillard) that was driven by an increased awareness of two facets of the crisis of the political Left. First, there was an increasing recognition that the reality of the Soviet Project for the creation of a more equal society was in reality becoming a terrifying distortion of Marx's conceived proletarian utopia. Reluctant as many were to admit it, Marxism, as presently articulated in the Soviet Union, appeared more horrific than any kind of capitalist alienation. But second, there was a growing recognition that the nature of the capitalist beast was itself changing. Baudrillard came to realize that conventional Marxism was proving increasingly inadequate to critique a form of capitalism in which the relationships between employer, labourer, commodity and consumer were all radically shifting. For the purposes of this book, these changes require some explanation.

The first half of the twentieth century can be seen as the culmination of the modern development of capitalism into its 'organized' industrial period. As industrial technology developed, commodities (steel, linen, corn, etc.) were produced to meet a functional need (*use-value*), but sold within a fluctuating market that dictated their price (*exchange-value*). Labour, too, functioned as the worker's own commodity, bought at a rate that enabled the employer to accumulate capital. In this period, these markets of commodity, capital and labour operated at a predominantly national level.[15] This characteristic was reinforced by the rise of democratic socialism which, as in the post-war Attlee Government in Great Britain, sought to redress the potentially 'poor deal' for the worker in this system by orienting production and its benefits towards the collective community of the nation state. This period saw the emergence of the large bureaucratic firm, operating by the logic of Fordist mass production and mass consumption; labour was divided to produce commodities on a large scale, often by a nationalized industry (British Steel, British Coal, British Motors, etc) for consumption in a largely national market. Trade unions too, no longer linked to locally based crafts and guilds, covered large sections of industry, lobbying national government to intervene in the interests of their members.

This development of 'organized' capitalism as a national and bureaucratic process is therefore characterized by a rigidly rational view in which the operations of the capitalist process are clearly defined to serve specified needs. Weber points out that the development of this formal rationality in capitalism was predicated upon the invention of accounting and bookkeeping, ensuring the possibility of rational control and prediction of these processes.[16] Within this 'contained' form of capitalism, supply meets demand, commodities satisfy needs through their use-value and the socialist concern that workers should be paid a fairer wage for their labour-power is met by state intervention in market processes.[17] In effect, while the Communist empire was seeking to enact the principle of 'from each according to their ability to each according to their need', western states were effectively seeking to do something similar through regulation of what they saw as the rational processes of the market: meeting needs through regulated production.

In the second half of the twentieth century, however, capitalism began to enter a new, 'disorganized' phase.[18] The circulation of capital, commodities and labour was emancipated from its national boundaries and accelerated within an increasingly global network.[19] With the deregulation of capital markets and the advent of mass communications, these flows of capital, commodities and information were also moving faster than had ever been imagined. This shift from an organized to a complex and accelerated capitalism brought with it a more significant shift. The commodity shifted from being the raw matter of capitalist production towards becoming a cultural phenomenon. The commodity is no longer the material object of the rational process of supply and demand, but an object of consumer desire. The locus of political economy has shifted from material to *cultural* production.

Baudrillard's early work is therefore particularly concerned with this new attention to the form of the postmodern commodity. Fundamentally, it is less governed by the producer and more by the need to respond to the consumer. The transition from the national to the global has meant that traditional production patterns of mass production and mass consumption have become more fragmented and flexible. National industries have been dismantled and the ethos of 'consumer choice' has done away with the 'one-size-fits-all' model of Fordist industry. Most significantly, this has resulted in a shift in the nature of *what* is being produced from substance (a material object that the consumer needs) towards signification (an object which 'says something' about or to the consumer). In effect, the commodity is becoming less often a material object so much as a *sign*, hence a new openness to the semiological anaylsis that Baudrillard undertakes in *The System of Objects* (1968). 'To become an object of consumption', he declares, 'an object must first become a sign'.[20]

This changing face of capitalism has resulted in the need for a new kind of discussion of political economy. It soon becomes clear that the traditional direction of relations between supply and demand, production and consumption, and the more negative questions of exploitation and alienation cannot be interpreted as coherently as before. This is the capitalism of the 'consumer society' in which the locus of political discourse has shifted from the means of production towards the circulation of cultural artefacts. Questions of need, desire, production and oppression now need to be posed within the context of a political economy that has colonized the cultural sphere with its emphasis on the visual signification and aesthetic expression. The politics of production has been replaced by the politics of the sign.

Situationalism was a significant philosophical attempt to respond to these transitions which had some influence on Baudrillard. In *Society of the Spectacle*, a text closely associated with the uprisings of 1968, Guy Debord set out a new theory of how consumer capitalism disempowers, not so much through its impositions of labour as through the alienation from reality itself by the bombardment of signs that this new form of production creates: 'In societies dominated by modern conditions of production, life is presented as an immense accumulation of spectacles. Everything that was directly lived has receded into a representation'.[21]

Debord's world is one in which reality is only accessible through media and he is nostalgic for a society in which the real world is most immediately accessed through touch. The consumer society has moved us into a world that can merely be *seen* and while it appears to be a good society its abundance masks the falseness of our choices and the impossibility of actually *altering* any of this spectacle. Visual culture is no longer simply a medium; it is the end in itself.[22] Liberal democracies have become dominated by the rhetoric of choice as the foundation of human freedom. Yet Debord and his colleagues argued that these choices were radically confined. The freedom and satisfaction of democratic late capitalism were simply the diffusing of revolution and disaffection through the play of signs. The Marxist dialectic of the empowered and the disempowered has been retained but the terminology of alienation has been shifted to the discussion of signs.[23]

Moving on from Marx

Baudrillard's earlier writings take a similar direction to Debord and are clearly influenced by him. His first two books, *The System of Objects* and *The Consumer Society* (1970), supplemented by his essays in *For a Critique of the Political Economy of the Sign* (1972), provide a similar account of the way in which the individual relates to the objective world in this new age of consumer capitalism. But these works represent the end of Baudrillard's allegiance to Marxist thought. In writing them he comes to perceive Marxism as an insufficiently radical form of thought to challenge the contemporary culture of production. Crucial to his argument at this stage is a deconstruction of the Marxist account of value generation and his uncovering of the inherently repressive agenda behind 'use-value'. To explain this fully requires a brief account of Marxist theory.

Marx's account of the logic of exploitation is quite specific; in the capitalist system, the use-values of commodities are exchanged in equivalence expressed in terms of their exchange-value (i.e. an object's utility is directly linked to the price it fetches in the market). Workers are exploited, however, because labour is the only commodity that does not receive a fair equivalence. In labour power, use-value exceeds exchange-value (i.e. employers get more from their workers than the workers are fairly rewarded for), and, conversely, Marx argues that capital is 'fetishized' since its exchange-value is disproportionate to its use-value.[24]

Baudrillard, however, asks the question, 'Where does use-value come from?' since, for Marx, it seems to be a kind of metaphysical quality. Marx thought that if the capitalist system with its logic of exchange were overthrown, use-value would remain as a definite, positive notion. Indeed, the foundational communist principle – 'to each according to his need' – is predicated on the idealist view that people's needs are clearly identifiable and satiable. Baudrillard suspects, however, that use-value is more culpably implicated in the capitalist system, and that this is increasingly the case in the shift from a production to a consumer-driven economy. Once society moves beyond the point of meeting very basic needs (enough food to live, clothing to protect from the cold, etc.) the question of what is 'useful' to meet a 'need' is far from obvious. In Western society, therefore, where destitution is all but eradicated, use-value is no longer objective, but neither is it fully subjective. Rather, it is generated by the system of desire: 'people discover a posteriori and almost miraculously that they need what is produced and offered at the marketplace'.[25]

Marx does not, therefore, take the cultural consequences of his theories as far as he should. His conviction that exchange-value is privileged over use-value as the driver of the system means that his analysis of the commodity does not fully appreciate the potency of its ideological form. This constitutes Marx's own lapse into ideology that use-values – and consequently utility and value themselves – are taken to be 'natural'. This logic of value is where Marx imports his own metaphysics:

> This is where we discover the real "theology" of value – in the order of finalities: in the "ideal" relation of equivalence, harmony, economy and equilibrium that the concept of utility implies. It operates at all levels: between man and nature, man and objects, man and his body, the self and others. Value becomes absolutely self evident, "la chose la plus simple". Here the mystery and cunning (of history and of reason) are at their most profound and tenacious.[26]

In order to explain contemporary political economy, Baudrillard considers an alternative value system: sign exchange-value. But this is more than the superstructural analysis of the kind we find in Roland Barthes' unpacking of the 'mythology' of signs.[27] Baudrillard takes Barthes' work further by drawing parallels between the breakdown of the relation between exchange-value and use-value and the more fundamental breakdown of the relation between the signifier and the signified in Saussurean theory. In both cases, the two poles appear to be operating in union (use-value underpinning exchange-value and the signified guaranteeing the signifier), but there is, in fact, an asymmetrical (and ideological) relation. Use-value is no more and exchange operates independently as a generalized, uncontrollable code. Similarly (as we shall see in more detail in the next chapter) the signified is lost to the signifier which now distorts reality through its codified interaction with other signs. The consumer object, the commodity, embodies the zenith of this distortion, achieving its meaning within the fluid arena of sign exchange rather than any concrete relation of use-value. Baudrillard writes:

> Like the sign-form, the commodity is a code managing the exchange of values. It is of little difference whether the material contents of material production or the immaterial contents of signification are involved; it is the code that is determinant: the rules of the game of signifiers and exchange value.[28]

In short, Baudrillard contends that within our context of 'fantastic conspicuousness of consumption and abundance, constituted by the multiplication of objects',[29] we no longer relate to objects in isolation but to the system (or code) as a whole. It is as if we are no longer consuming commodities so much as performing the idea (the system) of consumerism itself. Consistent with Saussure's semiological system, consumer goods find their meaning and signification within the whole vision of objects, a chain of signifiers.

Thus Baudrillard rejects traditional Marxism as merely 'the mirror of production'[30] that fails to take these new cultural/economic developments into account. In his fundamental rejection of primary use-value, he seeks to develop a new theory of political economy, 'the only one which today can recapture Marx's analysis on a global level'.[31] For him advanced capitalism does not serve human purposes or, in any real way, 'make sense'. It generates, of its own logic, signs that exert their own influence on us. With this rejection of utilitarian economic theories, Baudrillard posits that what we search for in the consumer society is the difference that the commodity represents within the whole order of signification that is consumerism. As such, the consumer system functions as a semiotic generator of meaning similar to language or the kinship rituals of primitive societies. In fact, Baudrillard views it as the primary semiotic system of our age, 'a system of signs which reveals itself to be one of the specific modes, and perhaps *the* specific mode, of transition from nature to culture in our era'.[32]

Baudrillard's semiological analysis of political economy is not without its critics. The cultural/semiotic turn of Marxist theory is even seen by some as a rather obtuse trivialization of Marx's quest for human freedom. Baudrillard's discussion of hyper-markets, Disneyland and fashion seems a far cry from the bold liberationist language of the Communist Manifesto. His subsequent criticisms of the traditional Left, his indifference and cynicism and his ultimate conclusion that we live in a 'transpolitical' age have led to criticisms of political naivety, even the accusation by Douglas Kellner that his project is a 'capitulation to the hegemony of the Right and a secret complicity with aristocratic conservatism'.[33] Such criticisms are not, in my view, without some justification. His indifferent tone is frequently maddening and he often appears dismissive of enduring political problems. But, equally, it is his move away from the strictures of Marxism and his willingness to think about the political and economic spheres with great imagination that cause his work to be of greater theological interest.

What Baudrillard embarks on at this early stage of his writing (in his 'break with Marxism') is an exploration of how the system of advanced capitalism, under which we live today, draws together the economic, social, cultural, philosophical and political dimensions of life in new and complex ways. Kellner concedes here that Baudrillard's work demonstrates that 'much established social theory and politics. . . is highly flawed, and fails to conceptualise the new social conditions and experiences of our epoch'.[34] Even basic political questions of what human freedom means become hard to answer as consumerism appears to offer a radical new definition of freedom (the one that now dominates the Western world). Baudrillard was one of the first to recognize the power of the new notion of liberation through choice that consumerism brought to capitalism, seeing it as the corollary of the 'liberty' of the worker's participation in the labour market:

> The capitalist system was erected on this liberty – one of the formal emancipation of the labour force (and not on the concrete autonomy of work, which it abolishes). Similarly consumption is only possible in the abstraction of a system based on the "liberty" of the consumer. It is *necessary* that the individual user have a choice, and become through his choice free at last to enter as a productive force in a calculus of production, exactly as the capitalist system frees the laborer to sell, at last, his labor power.[35]

Participation within the system of sign value has become the primary driver of human identity in much of the world today. As this passage indicates, of central concern to Baudrillard is the manner in which this generates the individual *as consumer* and fractures a more primal sense of communion which (as we shall see) he comes to identify with the symbolic exchange of primitive societies. Under sign value, the object 'begins to signify the abolition of the relationship'.[36] His early conviction of the sheer power and intensity of this circulation of signs and the inadequacy of traditional politics to counter it leads him to suggest that we have become strangers to reality itself. We are in a new era of simulation.

2

Simulation and the hyperreal

Everything is destined to reappear as simulation.[1]

Simulation is the idea most associated with Baudrillard. While he gives the theme little direct attention in his later work, it remains his foundational concept. In the late 1970s, Baudrillard set out his theory of a progressive descent into simulation that he called the 'precession of simulacra'. Essentially, this is the idea that our culture has become increasingly synthetic and artificial, losing contact with what we formerly knew to be real. In its final stage (hyperreality), simulation can be viewed as a totalized form of alienation, the state brought about by the dramatically accelerated capitalism discussed in the last chapter. This is a state in which the logic of capital, in its contemporary form of sign exchange, has replaced all meaningful human relations and taken us further and further away from a deep sense of human identity and social life. This chapter will set out Baudrillard's loose chronology of the 'precession of simulacra' and explore how simulation has resulted in the ascendency of a highly reductive form of thought and interaction, the 'metaphysics of the Code'. Finally the chapter will explore some preliminary religious implications of simulation.

Baudrillard's early formulation of simulation is comparable to the work of the Frankfurt School in its reflections on how advanced capitalism impacts on the way we live. He borrows from Herbert Marcuse the phrase that we live at 'the end of transcendence'[2] and in a state that Marcuse described as 'one dimensional'.[3] This formulation of the advanced capitalist predicament is also reminiscent of Michel Foucault's 'biopower'[4] in the way in which, through consumerism, capitalist processes have pervaded all aspects of everyday life and thought. This was the conclusion of his analysis of the consumer society:

> Commodity logic has become generalized and today governs not only labour processes and material products, but the whole of culture, sexuality, and human relations, including even fantasies and individual drives. Everything is taken over by that logic, not only in the sense that all functions and needs are objectivized and manipulated in terms of profit, but in the deeper sense in which everything is *spectacularized* or, in other words, evoked, provoked and orchestrated into images, signs and consumable models.[5]

In Baudrillard's thought, this culmination of capitalism in the age of radical alienation is closely associated with capitalism's *visual* turn, the shift from use to *sign*-value. The implications of this are not merely of interest to economics and sociology. As we shall see, Baudrillard believes that the fundamental assumptions of philosophy are no longer tenable as seemingly infinite reproduction creates a world where subjectivity and thought are themselves cut adrift from their former realities. In this radically fluid age, signs are now exchanged against each other rather than against any tangible reality. Just like the flotation of money in capital markets, needs, products, labour, even ideas, values and beliefs float as signs. Under consumer capitalism, 'the structural configuration of value simply and simultaneously puts an end to the regimes of production, political economy, representation and signs. With the code, all this collapses into simulation'.[6]

The order of simulacra

Baudrillard contends that this decay of the real into simulation has taken place in successive historical phases of simulacra: three elaborated in *Symbolic Exchange and Death* (1976) and four in *Simulacra and Simulation* (1981). The original order Baudrillard describes as 'sacramental', reflecting 'a theology of truth and secrecy'.[7] This was a time when signs had clear referents and the potential for symbolic meaning was great. This order is closely associated with symbolic exchange, which will be the subject of further discussion in the next chapter. It is an important recurring theme in Baudrillard's work, offering potential in the world of simulation for real communication and meaning. Symbolic exchange is the principle of sociality and communion. However, he veers between nostalgia for this original symbolic order and antipathy towards it. He certainly never laments the loss of what he calls 'the Real', as he retains the Marxist perspective that the social structures of reality in former eras have always been ideological and therefore repressive: 'If we take to dreaming once more – particularly today – of a world where signs are certain, of a strong "symbolic order", let's be under no illusions. . . In feudal or archaic caste societies, in *cruel* societies, signs are limited in number and their circulation is restricted'.[8] Examples of the kind of restriction Baudrillard means would certainly include the rare objects such as jewellery and books that were available only to the privileged classes in the Middle Ages. In the religious context we might draw parallels with the comparatively few occasions on which serfs and labourers would be permitted to receive the sacrament of Holy Communion. In this pre-modern order of signs, symbolic rites and objects of status were the preserve of the few.

The Renaissance sees the emergence of the first order of simulacra where traditional ranks and rituals are dismantled to allow wider social, democratic (and semiotic) participation. In this semiotic reading, the Sign too is emancipated and functions in more ambivalent and less traditionally symbolic ways. We see the 'emergence of overt competition at the level of signs of distinction'[9] through the advent of fashion trends and the wider availability of goods. This competition introduces to the semiotic order the idea of the *counterfeit*, a necessary consequence, Baudrillard argues, of 'a proliferation of signs according to demand'.[10] With the advent of the counterfeit, there is no longer an obligation of the sign in its reference to the real. The link between signifier and signified is already loosened. Nonetheless the link still exists, for the counterfeit can be a realistic copy or an artistic representation. Baudrillard therefore views the first order of simulacra as the classic age of the theatrical and representative arts, exemplified by stucco plaster decoration and *trompe-l'oeil* images. The great ambition of the Renaissance, he argues, was the imitation of nature via form, 'the transubstantiation of all nature into a single substance, a theatrical sociality unified under the sign of bourgeois values'.[11]

This evolved into the second order of simulacra, which was the order of production and the emergence of capitalism. Here the dialectic between the real and the simulacrum gradually erodes until there is no longer any analogy or reflection at all but an equivalence and indifference. This is the logic of exchange value, 'the market law of value'[12] that characterized the era of production. Transcendent, symbolic reference is gradually evacuated as the sign becomes pure commodity. 'No more semblance or dissemblance, no more God or Man, only an immanent logic of the principle of operativity'.[13] Signs have lost their symbolic efficacy and have changed 'with the advent of machines into crude, dull, industrial, repetitive, echoless, functional and efficient signs'.[14] With such commodified signs, the relation of signifier to signified collapses. In fact, all we are left with is a closed, self-referential system that is unable to make any reference to reality. Rather than providing any kind of representation of the real, the sign 'masks the *absence* of any profound reality'.[15] Baudrillard argues that 'reality' now merely provides the *alibi* for a sign that is free to play and manipulate our perception of what is real. As the sign is completely commodified, so it loses the link with its referent. All we now experience is a fluid semiotic construction of reality which Baudrillard labels the 'hyperreal'.

Within the hyperreal, representation is entirely replaced by simulation. Signs have become simulacra because they no longer have any reference to reality but generate their meaning (in the Saussurean manner) through their relation to one another. Baudrillard contends that reality is no longer imitated by the simulation but replaced by it, a process only made possible by the mass reproduction and mass media of the postmodern age. In these two spheres, he is heavily influenced by Walter Benjamin whose essay *The Work of Art in the Age of Mechanical Reproduction*[16] was the first to suggest that reproduction might itself absorb the processes of production. In this analysis of art, cinema and photography, Benjamin argued that mass-reproduced images would have a huge influence on the future construction of social and political life. A further influence was Marshall McLuhan who caught the spirit of our age in the slogan 'the medium is the message'.[17] For Baudrillard, these two thinkers saw more clearly than Marx that 'the real message, *the real ultimatum, lay in reproduction itself.* Production itself has no meaning: its social finality is lost in the series. Simulacra prevail over history'.[18] This has had a truly radical impact on the political and economic structures of our society as both spheres have degenerated into the same kind of low-level discourse:

> . . . propaganda and publicity were fused, marketing and merchandising both objects and powerful ideas. This linguistic convergence between the economic and political is moreover what marks a society such as ours, where 'political economy' has been fully realised. By the same token, it is also its end, since the two spheres are abolished in another reality or media hyperreality.[19]

Baudrillard's use of examples to provide evidence for his argument is sporadic and sometimes opaque. But part of the persuasiveness of his theories is that the twenty-first century world seems to present far better illustrations of the hyperreal than the 1970s and 1980s when he first set these theories down. Consider the way in which the contemporary brand functions in the global market. Today, signifiers such as 'Apple' or 'Nike' are good examples of hyperreal simulacrum. Obviously they continue to signify particular (though rapidly changing and diversified) products. But more central to their signification is their relation to and differentiation from other signifiers such as 'IBM', 'Microsoft', 'Adidas' and 'Puma'. There is then a wider play of signifiers that construct the (hyper)reality of the brand that include words such as 'alternative', 'revolutionary', 'superior', 'max' and 'performance'. And it is not merely the particular material products from which these constructed brands have become divorced. Other realities (and referents) have been lost. These may include the realities of developing world sweatshops and poor labour conditions. They may include the mineral conflicts perpetuated in countries like the Congo by demand for new technology. But we have also lost the sense that these brands should signify demystified commodities that should not confer status or human worth in the way our culture has come to believe. In the shift from use-value to sign-value the commodity has come to represent a redemptive object in our culture conferring a mythical (and temporary) value on the consumer. This is how consumerism has become a new and pervasive salvation narrative, not merely a 'retail therapy' but a 'retail soteriology'. This is what Baudrillard labels 'social salvation by consumption'.[20] Baudrillard's other famous example of hyperreality is another brand that has continued to expand its reach in recent decades: Disney. Disneyland represents 'a perfect model of all the entangled orders of simulacra' because here we see the intense interplay of unreal 'illusions and phantasms'.[21] But what he believes to be most attractive about Disneyland to the thousands who flock there is the fact that it is a parodic image of the country outside: 'the social microcosm, the *religious*, minaturised pleasure of the real America'.[22] The profile of America, its ideologies and values are all idealized and conserved in this capitalist theme park as a kind of utopian refuge from the true decay of all these things. But Disneyland is entirely simulacral because the relation between signifier and signified has gone. There is no longer a 'real' America to serve as the referent:

> Disneyland is presented as imaginary in order to make us believe that the rest is real, whereas all of Los Angeles and the America that surrounds it are no longer real, but belong to the hyperreal order and to the order of simulation. It is no longer a question of a false representation of reality (ideology) but of concealing the fact that the real is no longer real, and thus of saving the reality principle.[23]

Theme parks are thought to be the nonsense world that contrasts to the coherent world outside. But incoherence now pervades everyday life and adults come to the theme park to act the child 'in order to foster illusions as to their real childishness'.[24]

Baudrillard's narrative of the progressive degeneration of reality into simulation reads like a parody of Hegel's optimistic, progressive dialectic of history. His order of simulacra takes us from clarity and meaning to chaos and absurdity. To many of his critics, all this talk of the disappearance of reality in the age of the shopping mall seems like a facile distraction from the real business of politics and economics. Douglas Kellner, while conceding that the traditional political economy has radically changed, argues that Baudrillard has merely replaced it with a kind of 'sign fetishism'[25] that ignores present material relations, which continue to be dominated by capital. But Baudrillard contends that in our present form of capitalism, 'capital can never actually be grasped in its present reality' and the dynamics of power are more difficult to discern. 'By the time one phase has been unmasked, capital has already passed on to another . . . Capital cheats. It does not play by the rules of critique, the true game of history. It eludes the dialectic . . .'.[26]

In his accusation of 'sign fetishism', Kellner points to Baudrillard's underlying cynicism. His pronouncement of hyperreality is at times a counsel of despair, at others a charter for ambivalence. But it need not be so. As one of Baudrillard's obituary writers critically pointed out, 'We are participants in a public world, not hermits trapped in our own private cinemas. The cure for the sceptical nightmare is action'.[27] The complexity of today's financial and economic systems ought not to eradicate all sense of individual agency and accountability. Exploitation continues. But Baudrillard nonetheless depicts our more complex situation where the visual triumphs over transparent power relations and where higher virtues have been reduced to the low level desire of simulated, consumer life.

The metaphysics of the code

Hyperreality knows nothing of traditional metaphysics. As we have seen, this is an age without transcendence, an age where the proliferation of self-referential signs has excluded the possibility of depth and otherness. But neither is it an age of human emancipation from metaphysical control. Baudrillard contends that hyperreality is its own organizing superstructure that subordinates human freedoms. This is the metaphysics of the digital code with its binary systems and models:

> Cybernetic control, generation through models, differential modulation, feedback, question/answer, etc.: this is the new *operational* configuration (industrial simulacra being *mere operations*). Digitality is its metaphysical principle (Leibniz's God), and DNA is its prophet.[28]

Baudrillard's reference to Leibniz draws on McLuhan's understanding of this early theorist of logic and calculus as the one who 'saw in the mystical elegance of the binary system where only the zero and the one count, the very image of creation. The unity of the Supreme

Being, operating by means of a binary function against the nothing, was sufficient ground, he thought, from which all things could be made'.[29] Baudrillard sees the current pervasiveness of this binarism in the biological reductionism of DNA, the genetic code. He cites the American semiotician Thomas Sebeok's contention that the genetic code has today become 'the basic semiotic network' and, therefore, 'the prototype of all other systems of signification'.[30] This, Baudrillard argues, is an illusory and metaphysical attempt to systematize and 'decode' the whole material world (including the human being) in a way that pushes us further away from the real and reinforces the hyperreal: 'With Leibniz and his binary deity as their precursor, the technocrats of the biological (as well as the linguistic) sciences opt for the genetic code, for their intended programme has nothing to do with genetics, but is a social and historical programme'. This constitutes 'social control by means of prediction, simulation, programmed anticipation and indeterminate mutation, all governed, however, by the code'.[31]

Baudrillard sees codified, digital thought as the pervasive characteristic of hyperreal culture. Digitality 'haunts all the messages and signs of our society'.[32] To some degree, he views this as a mere extension of the emergence of binary oppositions in place of symbolic relations that may be seen as the means of social organization throughout the modern era (second order of simulacra): male and female, white people and black people and (most important to Baudrillard, as we shall discuss later) the living and the dead. However, in the third order of simulacra this binary form is manifest in all areas of life including the socio-political realm as citizenship is reduced from a symbolic form to the binarism of electoral participation. In today's social participation, the symbolic complexities (rites and rituals) of previous ages are replaced by binary impulses where the form of the 'referenda' (yes or no) is axiomatic. This reflects a commodification of political and social participation in a culture where all signs and messages present themselves to us as externalized question/answer signals, hence the predominance of 'choice' in consumer and contemporary political culture. All signs require the immediate response: 'Do I accept or reject this?', 'Is this "in" or "out"?', 'Do I want this or not?'. We consequently live our lives 'less as users than as readers and selectors, reading cells'.[33] But consonant with his rejection of use-value, Baudrillard insists that we do not have agency here; it is not us testing the sign, but the sign testing us, since choice is merely presented within a spectrum or range and so no choice is one that truly impacts upon and engages us. Particularly in the political sphere, the processes of polling and electoral quantification have reduced our political agency to operation within a network of selected questions dictated by pollsters, politicians, the media, a whole political culture. Fundamentally the meaning of 'the political' has been radically reduced by its codification. Questions which relate to the symbolic relations of politics (questions of political ideology) are becoming increasingly irrelevant: 'The entire political sphere loses its specificity as soon as it enters the media's polling game, that is to say, when it enters the integrated circuit of the question/answer. The electoral sphere is in any case the first large-scale institution where social exchange is reduced to getting a response'.[34]

It is therefore far from coincidental that the advanced capitalist countries are those in which an intractable two-party political system has emerged with very little real choice for voters. Choice in the consumer economy is always about alternation between essentially meaningless oppositions (do I buy Pepsi or Cola? McDonalds or Burger king? Are mini-skirts 'in' or 'out'?). Similarly political parties have become simulacra of their former ideologically based forms with minimal policy difference and affecting minimal change on the system. Elections merely regulate the political sphere through the alternation of forces in power in minority/majority substitutions: 'At the limit of pure representation, 'it' [ça] no longer represents anything. Politics dies from the over-regulated play of distinct oppositions. The political sphere (more generally, the sphere of power) is emptied'.[35]

Recent years have seen an even more dramatic increase in the use, not just of opinion polls, but the polling of public opinion by government through online e-petitions and by media outlets where viewers and listeners are encouraged to 'text in their views'. But is this discerning of public opinion through the binary interrogations of polling or the contribution of short statements of support or condemnation really a way in which the masses at large are drawn into political life and representation when the debate has such a tight frame of reference? The answer is surely no. Here Baudrillard turns again to Debord's visual theory: 'It is the burlesque spectacle of the hyperrepresentative (that is, not representative at all) political sphere that people savour and sample through opinion polls and the media'.[36] This 'nullité spectaculaire' and the reduction of political discourse into 'contemplation statistique' provokes fascination (as with the phenomenon of 24 hour political news coverage) but is inevitably accompanied by a profound disillusionment and political disengagement about which much is currently written and about which politicians (some at least) express much concern. Our political culture, in which agency is reduced to the consumer choices of polling and political discourse operates at the level of binary oppositions, seems destined to lead to profound disappointment.

The devastating effects of hyperreality on the social and political are further explored in Baudrillard's 1978 essay *In the Shadow of the Silent Majorities*. It paints a bleak picture of the post-materialist Western masses who 'absorb all the electricity of the social and political and neutralize it forever'.[37] As membership of trade unions, political parties and smaller community organizations decline, he describes how the drive towards organization and emancipation has been lost: the general population is 'a black hole which engulfs the social'.[38] On the one hand this essay feels like it has a snobbish tone, speaking condescendingly about the masses who prefer to watch football than engage in politics. On the other hand, it is undeniably realist and he castigates his former Marxist colleagues for their contemptuous interpretation that it is political authority that suppresses the masses: 'power manipulates nothing, the masses are neither misled nor mystified'.[39] It is not authority that has deconstructed the social but the logic of digitality which has turned the masses into 'a floating substance whose existence is no longer social, but statistical, and whose only mode of appearance is that of the survey'.[40] As the social has been colonized by the metaphysics of the Code, it has become 'a hyperreal, imperceptible sociality, no longer operating by law and repression, but by the infiltration of models'.[41]

While the focus of his arguments here are the revolutionary Left, his pessimistic view of the potential for social organization seems acutely relevant to recent debates in Britain about the need to overcome individualism to build a 'big society'. Baudrillard's essay seems quite prophetic in that we now seem to live in an age that recognizes the profound limitations of a political system that does not truly represent a population for whom wealth acquisition and consumerism have become the only ideologies of life. Renewal of social life is seen as the solution but the ultimate causes of the problem are the same: a deep social fragmentation. And so the underlying question remains the one that Baudrillard poses, 'what is to be done with these masses? They are the leitmotif of every discourse; they are the obsession of every social project; but all run aground on them, for all remain rooted in the classical definition of the masses, which is that of an eschatological faith in the social and its fulfillment'.[42]

This essay also marks Baudrillard's rejection of sociology since he contends that it is now impossible to submit the masses to any kind of analysis. The terms used to do so (class, social relations, power, status, institution) operate as constructs with no real referents. 'Sociology can only depict the expansion of the social and its vicissitudes . . . The reabsorption, the implosion of the social escapes it'. Sociology is incapable of grasping the gravity of our predicament. 'The hypothesis of the death of the social escapes it. The hypothesis of the death of the social is also that of its own death'.[43]

The idea of implosion is a theme Baudrillard develops in this essay, not simply in connection with the social. It is the inevitable consequence of the 'explosive' processes he sees through modernity, the expansion and explosion 'under the sign of universalised commerce, of economic and philosophical investments, under the sign of universal law and conquest'.[44] Through the acceleration of capitalism 'this explosive process has become uncontrollable, it has acquired a fatal speed or amplitude'[45] and so systems are imploding. Some are imploding violently and catastrophically such as through terrorism, which will be explored further in Chapter 6. Others are imploding smoothly and imperceptibly through impulses that are 'anti-universalist, anti-representative, tribal, centripetal'.[46] All forms of implosion concern the evacuation of meaning and a loss of the differentiation that characterized modernity.

The implosion of religion

Baudrillard's arguments focus primarily on the economic and political spheres, developing out of a Marxist analysis of political economy. But his theory of simulation and its implications for the way in which all reality is experienced in the contemporary world

impact on all areas of life and thought. We will briefly consider
here some of the preliminary implications of Baudrillard's thought
for theology and the Church. Baudrillard touches on these themes
himself, arguing that, at the dawn of the modern era, the process
of the hollowing-out of faith through the advances of human
reason led to an increasing recognition of the power (but ultimate
superficiality) of religious images, viewed in either fearful or
cynically manipulative terms. On the one hand, the iconoclasts
recognized this 'omnipotence of simulacra'[47] and reacted violently
to their sublimated fear 'that deep down God never existed, that
only the simulacra ever existed, even that God himself was never
anything but his own simulacrum'.[48] The opposing reaction (which
Baudrillard identifies with the counter-Reformation Jesuits) is that
of a cynical embrace of this empty performance. This is theology
and liturgy founded on 'the virtual disappearance of God and
on the worldly and spectacular manipulation of consciences –
the evanescence of God in the epiphany of power – the end of
transcendence, which now only serves as an alibi for a strategy
altogether free of influences and signs'.[49]

Baudrillard's argument is controversial in his complete denial
that core religious *belief* acts today (or in the past) as any kind of
unitive force. He insists that it is ritual rather than doctrine that has
always attracted people to religion. In *The Silent Majorities* he cites
God as the best example of the impossibility of the circulation of
ideas among the masses:

> They have never been affected by the Idea of God, which has
> remained a matter for the clergy, nor by anguish over sin and
> personal salvation. What they have retained is the enchantment
> of saints and martyrs; the last judgment; the Dance of Death;
> sorcery; the ceremony and spectacle of the Church; the immanence
> of ritual . . . They were and have remained pagans . . . [50]

His tone is ambivalent as he describes this caricature of religion.
On the one hand, he seems to retain the disdain of his Protestant
background for the 'fantastic distortion of the religious principle'
that this represents. On the other, he seems also to celebrate this
popular rejection of ideas over spectacle: 'For the masses, the
Kingdom of God has always been already here on earth, in the

pagan immanence of images, in the spectacle of it presented by the Church'.[51]

Baudrillard was not alone in seeing this process of the 'hollowing-out' of religion as having taken place for quite some time. Feuerbach writes a strikingly similar critique of sacramental worship in the preface to the second edition of *The Essence of Christianity*. He defines his era (the mid-nineteenth century) as one which 'prefers the sign to the thing signified, the copy to the original, fancy to reality, the appearance to the essence, this change, inasmuch as it does away with illusion, is an absolute annihilation, or at least a reckless profanation; for in these days *illusion* only is *sacred, truth profane*'.[52] The implications of this in his analysis of Christianity are, for him, clear:

Religion has disappeared, and for it has been substituted, even among Protestants, the *appearance* of religion – the Church – in order at least that "the faith" may be imparted to the ignorant and indiscriminating multitude; *that* faith being still the Christian, because the Christian churches stand now as they did a thousand years ago, and now, as formerly, the *external signs* of the faith are in vogue. That which has no longer any existence in faith (the faith of the modern world is only an ostensible faith, a faith which does not believe what it fancies that it believes, and is only an undecided, pusillanimous unbelief) is still to pass current as *opinion*: that which is no longer sacred in itself and in truth is still at least to *seem* sacred. Hence the simulated religious indignation of the present age, the age of shows and illusion, concerning my analysis, especially of the Sacraments.[53]

Baudrillard locates this thinning of religious meaning in an earlier period, but it was during the nineteenth century with its huge advances in scientific discovery and the social upheaval of industrialization, when Christian practice became most disengaged from the world. We could say that Christianity in Western Europe became a simulacral practice as it retreated into idealist form. In seeking to re-enchant a world being spiritually deconstructed by rationalism, evolution and mechanization, the Church simply let go of evolving realism. Indeed, many of the revivalist movements, of both the Evangelical and Tractarian kind, attracted popularity at the expense of engagement with culture. Gouldstone labels this the 'aestheticization of faith', a retreat into the external practice of faith 'at the cost of undervaluing unanswered questions raised by science, materialism and the dark agnosticism that shadows all faith'.[54] He sees this as enduring today in the Church's preoccupation with 'heritage' to which one might also add the dominance of an individualized and experiential kind of 'spirituality'. What underpins both of these is sentiment and sentimentality.

In the present age, the dangers of simulacral religious practice are widespread. There has been a shift in many of the world faiths towards particular visual signs of religious affiliation (the hijab in Islam, the kippah in Judaism, the turban in Sikhism). Recent legal test cases of anti-Christian discrimination in the UK have concerned the right to wear a cross in the workplace, a visual statement never previously considered a religious requirement. The need to defend religious signs in the visual realm is perhaps indicative of a complex age when it is no longer easy to map deeper religious identity onto the shape of social, family and personal life. As in the political sphere, the visual message is substituted for reflection on substantial content. This is no doubt fed in many quarters by a shift in discussion of religious affairs into the virtual world of online networks. Complex questions are reduced to binary oppositions and popular disputes (now operating at a global level), exacerbated through lack of face-to-face encounter. In the thoroughly 'deregulated' world of advanced capitalism, the loss of the traditional rhythms and disciplines in the practice of faith can expose an emptiness at the heart of our devotional practice. Polarized disputes provide both a distraction and a perverted sense of purpose, which hide the fear that beneath our squabbling over secondary issues our faithful attention to primary theological questions is in a deep malaise.

Simulacral religious community is plagued by an ironic self-perception and an unarticulated realization that it fails to live up to the things that it says about itself. Slavoj Žižek identifies this as the universal characteristic of the post-ideological universe that 'we perform our symbolic mandates without assuming them and "taking them seriously"'. This is made possible by a constant flow of ironic, cynical and reflexive comments about our behaviour. Within this 'flattened' universe, evacuated of transcendence, Žižek sees a paradoxical inversion of human fear: 'we are afraid to discover not that we are mortal but, rather, that we are *immortal*'.[55] The German theologian Johann Baptist Metz identified a comparable cynicism at

work in today's Church when he asked, 'Do not Christians present
to the world the embarrassing spectacle of a people who speak of
hope, but do not actually hope for anything anymore?'[56] Perhaps it
is even worse than this; perhaps our talk of hope masks the real fear
that what we say we believe is actually true.

3

Exchange: Economic and symbolic

There is an order of exchange and an order of fate.[1]

The previous chapter considered Baudrillard's core idea of simulation and the degeneration of the social into hyperreality through the metaphysics of the Code. This chapter turns to Baudrillard's understanding of exchange (between subject and object, between human beings) and its relation to the complex notion of the 'fatal'. We will consider both the debasement of exchange through its 'generalization' within the closed system of the hyperreal and the enduring possibilities of exchange in the symbolic and its later variant, 'seduction'.

Fatality and totality

Human society is constituted by processes of exchange: the giving and receiving of things as an expression of human social life. We tend to think of this today simply in terms of a transactional economic exchange, the exchange of goods for capital. But different societies have had many forms of exchange, including the social or ritual exchange of non-material goods such as prestige and affection. In addition, many societies have had different forms of economic material exchange too, including bartering or less rational transactions, as we shall come on to discuss. Under capitalism, however, all forms of material exchange have been reduced to a transactional exchange: both commodities and labour sold in exchange for capital. Furthermore, as capitalism has moved into its disorganized phase, immaterial things have also been drawn into these processes of economic transactional exchange: debt, risk, brands, ideas and concepts. Consequently, more and more of our lives are governed by a transactional exchange governed by the logic of the market.

The possibility of market exchange presupposes some kind of equivalence (i.e. everything can be defined in terms of monetary value), hence Baudrillard sees our age as characterized by a general 'logic of equivalence'. Transactional exchange has become the ground of our morality, 'the idea that everything can be exchanged, that the only thing that exists is what can assume value, and hence pass from one to another'.[2] Thus under hyperreality, all modes of exchange are subsumed into a *generalized* exchange, the exchange of flows, of networks, of universal communication. This total commodification, total fluidity, has the effect of eradicating value: 'zero degree of value in total equivalence'.[3]

In the previous chapter, we saw how this has brought about the death of the Social. Yet, like Foucault, Baudrillard's most significant philosophical move is to declare that the velocity and intensity of these processes of generalized exchange lead to the death of the human subject itself. The hyperreality of postmodernity is far worse than the 'death of God' which Nietzsche saw in modernity: it is the death of the god that replaced him – the social, political, revolutionary human subject: 'when God died, there was still Nietzsche to say so . . .'.[4] How are we to understand this extreme declaration of the end of human subjectivity? In the first instance, one might say that, in this hyperreal era, technology has generated a virtual simulated world into which people flee from the 'desert of the real'. The internet, new media and technological experience absorb more and more of people's time and, according to Baudrillard, our very personhood.[5] We can no longer speak of our computers as entirely external objects; we too are becoming part of the machines we have created. In an essay describing the current human condition as 'screened out', Baudrillard writes, 'The computer is a true prosthesis. I am not merely in an interactive relationship with it, but a tactile intersensory relation. I become, myself, an ectoplasm of the screen'.[6] Technology begins to engulf human subjectivity as we know it.

But eventually in Baudrillard's reading of the relation between subject and object, a fundamental *reversal* takes place. Baudrillard concluded his early work *The System of Objects* with the claim that 'there are no more [political, social or revolutionary] projects – only objects'.[7] This idea is taken to its extreme conclusion in *Fatal Strategies*, where one understanding of the 'fatality' referred to in the title is that of the human subject amid the new supremacy of the object. At the end of the long history of modernity where we have 'lived off the splendor of the subject and the poverty of the object'[8] the roles have reversed and the object is now king, such that, 'Today, the position of the subject has become simply untenable. No one today can be assumed as the subject of power, knowledge or history . . . The entire destiny of the subject passes into the object'.[9]

It is worth pointing out that the irony of Baudrillard's own position becomes apparent here. He shares the problematic of all critical theorists who seek to take the role of analysing observer within the system they seek to critique. However, this tension is particularly acute for Baudrillard since his social critique centres on both the impossibility of anything standing outside the advanced capitalist system of sign exchange and the neutralization of everything within it. Agency becomes radically impossible. All things, people and ideas become signs that constitute and perpetuate the System. The political and social spheres in which we seek to operate are a closed world where opportunities for decisive action and creative imagination are fatally restricted.

In his early work, Baudrillard demonstrates this 'closed system' by showing how, under advanced capitalism, seemingly opposing concepts are in fact indispensable to one another. Their opposition is held in constant tension rather than moving their dialectic forward as Hegel sought to argue in his role of the negative.[10] Consequently, the human drive to eliminate the negative element in order to bring about some kind of betterment is futile. An early attempt to show this is found in Baudrillard's discussion of 'waste' in *The Consumer Society*, a theme he takes up from Georges Bataille. From the perspective of our own time, 30 years on from Baudrillard's writing, it is perhaps difficult to remember what a cultural shift the move towards the 'throwaway society' has been.[11] Within a generation, post-war culture, conditioned by rationing and economizing, had given way to a mentality of the radical transience of all commodities. We accept that clothes will soon become outdated and technology will quickly become redundant. It is easy to forget that this development was unforeseen and for a long time ignored, since it exposes the reality that consumerism provides us with a lot of things that we do not really need[12] and that the problem of disposing of waste will become ever more intractable.

However, when use-value was still viewed as the benchmark of consumer theory, waste was viewed as something opposed to consumption, an obstacle to its proper functioning, since fundamentally waste is 'useless' and unmarketable. Still today the moral discourse among environmentalists and advocates of recycling is the constant call for a reining-in of waste, viewing it as 'a kind of madness, of insanity, of instinctual dysfunction, which causes man to burn his reserves and compromise his survival conditions by irrational practice'.[13] Baudrillard argues for the futility of the environmentalists' cause by inverting this logic in a way that is much more readily recognizable today. He suggests that waste is not inconsistent with the consumer system, rather *the system is founded upon it.* Conspicuous waste, particularly the wasteful extravagance of celebrities presented to us in the media, serves the function of providing the economic stimulus for mass consumption. Baudrillard's definition of consumption therefore takes on a sense of 'consummation'. An object's destruction is part of its use; it is invested with an immediate 'eye to death'. Thus waste and destruction are integral components of the system:

> destruction remains the fundamental alternative to production: consumption is merely an intermediate term between the two . . . It is clear that destruction, either in its violent and symbolic form (the happening, potlatch, destructive acting-out, both individual and collective) or in its form of systematic and institutional destructiveness, is fated to become one of the preponderant functions of post-industrial society.[14]

This is a fundamentally important argument for Baudrillard since it is a more universal truth for him that negativity does not challenge or drive forward a system as in Hegelian philosophy. Rather it is in-built to the system. This is the nature of the totality. An inevitable entropic process is taking place and we should be wary of naively assuming that the system can be improved through the eradication of its negative aspects. Baudrillard takes the socialist policy of wealth redistribution, a perceived means of eradicating the 'negativity' of poverty, to further illustrate this point. Taxation is always thought of as a means of righting the inequalities that arise within the system, lubricating the mechanisms of the market in distributing wealth more fairly between rich and poor. Taxation's failure to achieve any lasting success with regard to these goals generates constant debates about effective spending of public money (in fact this has now supplanted levels of taxation as the main subject of debate between the major political parties). But Baudrillard turns this logic on its head to suggest that it is precisely in this apparent inefficiency of redistribution that taxation serves its purpose. Taxation creates the framework for consumption, creating the differentiation that drives consumer desire. Consumerism could not function in an economically undifferentiated society so public spending and, in particular, social security create a kind of 'social inertia'. Rather than addressing inequality, taxation maintains it at a certain level to perpetuate consumerism.[15]

Baudrillard's analysis is contentious here, but it is undeniable that a certain amount of his realism about social inequality and income differentials has been absorbed into political culture since he was writing. In the climate of 1970s France (with the combination of the confident statism of President Pompidou's Gaullism and the post-1968 socialist resurgence), there was a much more sincere confidence in redistributive taxation policies to bring about a more equal 'New Society'.[16] The rise of free market forces has fundamentally challenged this kind of idealism while, paradoxically, rarely bringing about any reduction in public spending and state intervention.[17] Consequently, as Baudrillard points out, the payment of large social security budgets to bring about little structural social change is the most contentious (and intractable) political issue of our time. Perhaps in the twenty-first century it is even easier to see the evidence for Baudrillard's argument that 'the mechanisms of redistribution, which are so successful in preserving privilege, are in fact an integral part, a tactical element, of the power system'.[18]

So already in this early work, Baudrillard depicts our predicament as one of a totalized, codified system where human agency to bring about change is radically restricted. This restriction of human subjectivity is taken to a new paradigm as he describes the world in terms of the simulated abstractions explored in the previous chapter. The metaphysics of the Code draws human identity itself into its deconstructive logic. As we shall come to see, the loss of the human is, for Baudrillard, very much the loss of the *relational* human. Thus, the death of the human goes hand in hand with the processes of generalized exchange, the codification and simulation of all human relations:

> The loss of (spontaneous, reciprocal, symbolic) human relations is the fundamental fact of our societies. It is on this basis that we are seeing the systematic reinjection of human relations – in the form of *signs* – into the social circuit, and we are seeing the *consumption* of those relations . . . in *signified form*.[19]

In his later work, Baudrillard comes to describe this kind of closed system as 'integral reality'. The extension of the Code of the hyperreal takes human relations into an atemporal, highly visual realm as part of 'the perpetrating on the world of an unlimited operational project whereby everything becomes . . . visible and transparent, everything is "liberated"'.[20] These are the human relations constituted by social networks such as Facebook, virtual relationships where the dimensions of time and space necessary to human life and relationship have been eradicated in a virtual real time: 'If there were a subject of history, a subject of knowledge, a subject of power, these have all disappeared in the obliteration by real time of distance, of the pathos of distance, in the integral realization of the world by information'.[21] It is in this kind of virtual world that we can speak of the death of the human.

Symbolic exchange

Baudrillard's use of the word 'fatal', however, has a second, contrasting meaning. It derives from the word 'fate' in the sense that it suggests events and encounters over which the human subject cannot have any control. As such, in Baudrillard's language, the fatal points to something more primary in human relations and represents the new possibilities that emerge precisely at the moment of the death of the subject and the supremacy of the object. The concept of the autonomous human individual was in any case, for Baudrillard, a product of the modern era and a symptom of already fractured human relations. It is, therefore, once this illusory subject is lost that new possibilities of sociality can emerge:

What is fascinating then – what makes that moment an event –
is that a mode of sociality can be created which is not the mode of
exchange but occurrence of pure events . . . We live in a world that
is very loose, quite lax, in which things are more or less arbitrary,
disconnected and therefore sporadic, erratic. The order of the
fatal, on the other hand, is the site of symbolic exchange.[22]

Throughout his work, in opposition to digitality and the
metaphysics of the Code, Baudrillard contrasts a symbolic mode
of relation which operates on a more complex, multi-layered and
ambivalent level. It is this 'symbolic exchange', with the potential
to stand outside of simulation, that Baudrillard sets out in *For a
Critique* and further develops in *Symbolic Exchange and Death*.
Baudrillard later explained that this is a concept he borrowed
from anthropology as a deconstructive tool: 'The point for me in
using this concept was to take the opposite stance from commodity
exchange and, in that way, make a political critique of our society in
the name of something that might perhaps be dubbed utopian, but
that has been a living concept in many other cultures'.[23]

So rather than the Symbolic Order used by Lacan in psychoanalysis, this symbolic exchange is derived from the anthropological tradition of Levi-Strauss and Marcel Mauss whose theory of
gift-exchange in primitive societies proved, for Baudrillard, more
radical in the long term than Freud or Marx.[24] Mauss' *The Gift:
The Form and Reason for Exchange in Archaic Societies* carried
out pioneering work into the forms of exchange exhibited in primitive North-western Native American societies. His central notion
is that of the 'potlatch', a system of gift-giving in which the honour
of the agents involved was engaged in a way that is totally alien
to the value logic of market exchange. According to Mauss, the
potlatch was a key component in the system of 'total services', a
complexity of permanent quasi-contracts between clans by which
wealth and services were transferred. Exchange in this system is
characterized by three obligations: the obligation to give, the obligation to receive and the obligation to reciprocate. Thus the system
can be characterized as gift→reception→return-gift. The extent to
which this process is different to the exchange logic of capitalism
is sometimes underestimated. No equivalence of value is at play
and there is no need to be suspicious of the extent to which the
initial gift is given 'for nothing'.[25] In contrast to our own ethos of

possession and quantified exchange, in these societies 'one hastens to give. There is not one single, special moment . . . when one is not obliged to invite one's friends, to share with them the windfall gains of the hunt or food gathering'.[26] It is in response to the reception of this generosity that further generosity is prompted: 'the obligation to reciprocate worthily is imperative'.[27]

Significantly, this system brought object-exchange into direct relation with festival and ritual, a theme further explored by Georges Bataille, on whom Baudrillard may have drawn significantly. Associating it with occasions such as initiations, marriages and funerals, Bataille argues that the potlach 'cannot be separated from a festival; whether it provides the occasion for this festival, or whether it takes place on the festival's occasion'.[28] What is of fundamental interest here is that, in the social exchange of a festival (and in stark contrast to the binary exchanges of the sign economy), the status of the agents changed as much as the status of the object. Baudrillard sees the transition to a sign economy as the substitution of symbols with signs: 'In symbolic exchange, of which the gift is our proximate illustration, the object is not an object: it is inseparable from the concrete relation in which it is exchanged, the transferential pact that it seals between two persons'.[29] But, lest one is tempted to become too sentimental about symbolic exchange, this form of exchange is always complex and ambivalent – there is both *presence* and *absence*:

> [The giver of the symbolic gift] divests himself as if of part of himself – an act which is significant in itself as the basis, simultaneously, of both the mutual presence of the terms of the relationship, and their mutual absence (their distance). The ambivalence of all symbolic exchange material (looks, objects, dreams, excrement) derives from this: the gift is a medium of relation *and* distance; it is always love and aggression.[30]

The importance of this darker dimension of *absence* in symbolic exchange becomes the focus of Baudrillard's writing in *Symbolic Exchange and Death* where he argues that a central theme in the transition from symbolism to sign exchange is the increasing exclusion of the dead from social ritual. Following Foucault's genealogies of crime and punishment, sex and madness, Baudrillard attempts a 'genealogy of death' in which he charts the progressive ejection of the dead from symbolic circulation. Little by little, *the dead cease to exist* until the point where 'today, *it is not normal to be dead*, and this is new. To be dead is an unthinkable anomaly; nothing else is as offensive as this'.[31] Primitive societies, he argues, had no biological concept of death. Rather it was understood (like the body) as a social relation. Modern societies have de-socialized death by according it the immunity of science and giving it the autonomy of 'individual fatality'. Here Baudrillard concedes that Christian ritual of death retained an important social dimension: 'The priest and the extreme unction still bore a trace of the community where death was discussed. Today, blackout'.[32]

The rituals of primitive societies performed the function 'neither to conjure death away, nor to 'overcome' it, but to articulate it socially'.[33] Baudrillard gives the example provided by Robert Jaulin in *La Mort Sara* (1967) of an initiation ceremony where the ancestral group 'swallow the *koys*' (young initiation candidates) who die *symbolically* in order to be reborn. This ritual forms 'an incessant play of responses where death can no longer establish itself as end or as agency'.[34] The important moment is when the *moh* (grand priests) symbolically put the *koy* to death so that they are consumed by their ancestors, then the earth gives birth to them as their mother had given birth to them. After having been 'killed', the initiates are left in the hands of their initiatory 'cultural' parents who instruct them, care for them and train them:

> The uninitiated child has only been born biologically, he has only one 'real' father and one 'real' mother; in order to become a social being he must pass through the symbolic event of the initiatory birth/death, he must have gone through the circuit of life and death in order to enter into the symbolic reality of exchange.[35]

So we can see again the double meaning of Baudrillard's fatal strategies. To rediscover our 'fate' is to rediscover something of this ambivalent symbolic exchange of presence and absence, to move beyond collapse into the signs of hyperreality. But to do that is also to re-examine our society's exclusion of death, both re-articulating it symbolically in the manner described above (this theme will be returned to in Chapter 5) and learning to embrace its reality as a gift to be both received and given (discussed in Chapter 6). Jacques Derrida has argued along similar lines, 'In order to put oneself to death, to give oneself death in the sense that every relation to death is an interpretative apprehension and a representative approach to death, death must be taken upon oneself. One has to give it to oneself by taking it upon oneself, for it can only be mine alone, irreplaceably'.[36] But Derrida's emphasis on individual autonomy here ('giving it to oneself') is in stark contrast to Baudrillard's insistence that death is a social relation that must be articulated socially and not simply received personally. This difference, perhaps betraying Derrida as a 'post-existentialist' and Baudrillard as a 'post-structuralist', highlights the particular centrality of exchange in Baudrillard's thought and we will return to this crucial difference in Chapter 10.

Before leaving this discussion of symbolic exchange, it should be noted that Baudrillard's appropriation of Mauss' ethnographic analysis is not unproblematic methodologically and may frequently look like a misplaced nostalgia.[37] This danger was already present in *The Consumer Society* where he draws on the work of Marshall Sahlins to contrast the social logic of *scarcity* that dominates the consumer society with the primitive nomadic tribes of Australia and the Kalahari, 'who, in spite of their absolute "poverty", knew true affluence' since 'in the economy of the gift and symbolic exchange, a small and always finite quantity of goods is sufficient to create general wealth'.[38] The questions this raises for our understanding of development and human flourishing will be discussed in Chapter 7. But for now we should remind ourselves that Baudrillard's use of the potlatch is more polemical than constructive. Mauss' work enables him to point a different understanding of society and a different mode of exchange to the one that presently dominates our imagination. Thus he is able to help us imagine that there might be another way for human beings to live.

As such, his appropriation of 'lost societies' can be seen as quasi-theological in providing a partial vision of a way of being that has yet to be fully articulated. Born out of the 'fatality' of the all-powerful post-Enlightenment human subject, symbolic exchange points to the rediscovery of a patterning of human relationship ordered by a 'fate' that is beyond our commodified way of life, ordered by the operations of the market. Baudrillard speaks of his fatal strategies in terms of 'going over to the side of the object'. This need not merely imply a cynical embracing of our consumer culture, where the commodity object reigns supreme. It implies, for example, the new ways of thinking emerging in science (such as quantum mechanics) where 'microscopic observation provokes such an alteration in the object that knowledge of it becomes imperilled'.[39] It implies 'a delusive, illusive, allusive strategy'[40] from the object of 'the masses' who will occasionally defy the opinion polls and the codified regulation of their lives. In Chapter 5 I will explore Baudrillard's assertion that this kind of 'fatal strategy' is experienced through participation in ritual and ceremony and in Chapter 10 I will suggest that it may even be read as a theological strategy of going over to the divine Other.

Seduction

Symbolic exchange remains one of Baudrillard's principal motifs throughout his writing. But he also draws on other terms to invoke the ambivalence and 'reversibility' of the symbolic order that challenges simulation and market exchange. Principal among these is 'seduction', a way of thinking that, for Baudrillard, 'stands out radically against the universe of production'.[41] If symbolic exchange drew primarily on anthropology, seduction is more influenced by psychoanalysis, or rather its decline as a source for the rational interpretation of human behaviour:

> One may catch a glimpse of another, parallel universe (the two never meet) with the decline of psychoanalysis and sexuality as strong structures . . . a universe that can no longer be interpreted in terms of psychic or psychological relations, nor those of repression and the unconscious, but must be interpreted in terms of play, challenges, duels, the strategy of appearances – that is in terms of seduction.[42]

The complex arguments Baudrillard makes about seduction in relation to women and sexuality will be discussed further in Chapter 8. But it is important to note that seduction is not limited to its conventional sense. It parallels symbolic exchange in that Baudrillard sees it not only as a theme present in the working of consumer society (the pervasiveness of 'sex appeal' is obvious) but more fundamentally as a primal, primitive and subversive force.

Much of Baudrillard's discussion of seduction concerns the play of appearances and form (once again *trompe l'oeil* features as a favourite motif), reflecting how seduction operates in a society that has become reduced to the visual. Thus it is also a 'fatal strategy' of going over to the object. In the consumer society it is the object that seduces, that draws us beyond the realm of production into a more complex play of forms, particularly the reversal of power relations. In Baudrillard's seemingly confusing and provocative use of this term, seduction should be understood essentially as the play of forms to generate a symbolic relation. He argues that production, in the visual culture, takes to the extreme, the enlightenment project of 'unmasking' in a way that reduces human interaction to the transactional. In contrast, seduction implies a kind of masking, a return to the secretive and enigmatic. This is, of course, present in the conventional meaning of a seduction where a complex relation is formed between two people and attraction is created as much by what is concealed about the other as what is made present.

However, this process of masking and attracting to subvert transaction exchange and conventional power relations underpins Baudrillard's broader understanding of seduction. In a society that has become over-exposed and, therefore, 'obscene', seduction constitutes a 'scene' that resists the reductions of generalized exchange. While our culture has come to praise absolute 'transparency' as a means of accountability and the right to 'expose' as a sign of liberation, Baudrillard advocates seduction, not as some sort of 'cover-up' in either sense, but as the reclaiming of a space for symbolic relations to reform (I consider poetry as the opposite to pornography in this context in Chapter 9). That may be in the political, social or personal arenas.

But it should be clear that seduction is more than simply some sort of visual game. Like symbolic exchange it points to a new kind of social ordering and so is considered 'the original crime' that the reductionism of digitality and hyperreality seek to eradicate:

> Our attempts to positivize the world, to give it a unilateral meaning, like the immense undertaking of production, are no doubt aimed at abolishing this ultimately dangerous, 'evil' terrain of seduction. For this world of forms – seduction, challenge, reversibility – is the more powerful one. The other,

the world of production, has power; but potency, for its part, lies with seduction . . . And all types of production are perhaps subordinate to it.[43]

Thus *Seduction* explores modes of exchange that Baudrillard considers more powerful than the social regulation of market exchange. It covers similar material to *Symbolic Exchange and Death* of ritual and ceremony, games and their rules and the body as the primary site of this defiance. Much of this seems very conjectural, but an interesting area that Baudrillard explores to distinguish between codified society and seduction is the difference between a sociality bound by laws and the one bound by rules. His argument is that rules (as an expression of seduction) are far more powerful and cohesive. 'You can do anything with the law. With the rule, on the other hand, either you play or you don't play. If you play, the rule is implacable'. Again, it is this transparency in codification that has a weakening effect, since a rule is 'secret, never known, never spoken. If it were known, things would become visible and reversible again'.[44] As our society becomes more and more litigious, where rights and responsibilities are increasingly set down, Baudrillard points to the fact that rules of social convention (the 'rules of the game') will always be more powerful. Perhaps, for example, the attraction of gang membership to disaffected young people today lies in the strength of a sociality bound together by rules rather than a law-based society from which they feel excluded and in which there is little symbolic ritual to cement their participation. The core sense of 'attraction' signified by the word 'seduction' leads us to ask what it is in a society of generalized exchange that attracts people to one another – attracts them to social participation – rather than simply attracts them to further material acquisitiveness.

Baudrillard has been dismissed both for his creative use of the anthropology of symbolic exchange and his 'aristocratic'[45] appropriation of the themes considered under the heading of seduction. But, consistent with his self-description as a mystic and a metaphysician, they should be considered conceptual resources for imagining a world that is not governed by the reductionist systems of transactional exchange, digitality, hyperreality and the virtual. Perhaps they are not so far from Jesus' parables which offer incomplete images and ideas to feed our imaginations: 'The Kingdom of God is like . . . '. And like the parables, Baudrillard himself suggests that their vision will not be realized by any human system but must await some consummation beyond. '[The Fatal] cannot be deciphered or interpreted. The subject has nothing to say about it. Events emerge from any and every place, but from an absolute beyond, with that true strangeness which alone is fascinating'.[46]

4

Life after God

*God has departed, but he has left his judgement behind,
the way the Cheshire Cat left his grin.*[1]

The previous two chapters have set out the essentials of Baudrillard's
thought as it developed through the 1970s and 1980s. By the 1990s,
his work had been translated into many languages and he began to
attain celebrity status as the so-called 'high priest of postmodernity'.
While Baudrillard rarely used the terms postmodern or postmodernity, his later writings have come to exemplify this genre of writing
that looks critically, if also ironically and ambivalently, at the highly
complex world of advanced capitalism and far-reaching technology in which we live. He challenges orthodoxy in many disciplines,
adopting a frequently unscholarly, idiosyncratic mode of writing
that draws as much from popular culture as from formal theory.
His own writing is 'implosive', collapsing traditional disciplinary
boundaries and principles of reason to think our contemporary predicament in new ways.

If the world Baudrillard describes is a difficult world for
theologians to engage with it is perhaps because of the link he
perceives between our conceptions of God and the 'reality principle'
of modernity, a reality he now believes to have entirely disappeared
into hyperreality. The traces of this modern God continue to
surround us, both in terms of enduring delusions of reason and
contemporary resurgence of religion: 'For if the hypothesis of God
has disappeared – if He is indeed dead, as Nietzsche said – we still
have to deal – now, and for a long time to come – with His ghost
and His metastases'.[2] But as I hope subsequent chapters of this

book will show, Baudrillard also opens up ways of thinking about God that need not be so 'cancerous'. This chapter sets out some of his later ideas, preparing the ground for subsequent theological reflection.

Impossible exchange

The (a)theological implications of our descent into the hyperreal are most clearly set out in the first chapter of *Impossible Exchange* (1999). This is a series of reflections on what it means to live in the age when 'the sphere of the real is itself no longer exchangeable for the sphere of the sign'.[3] This is the impossible exchange referred to in the title: the fact that all systems operate self-referentially and nothing can be seen as truly representative of anything else. 'No equivalent, no double, no representation, no mirror . . . so there can be no verifying of the world'. This is true of all spheres – politics, law, economics, culture – all have lost any sense of reference to something beyond themselves such as ideological or philosophical grounding, absolute values or principles: 'Literally, they have no meaning outside themselves and cannot be exchanged for anything. Politics is laden with signs and meanings, but seen from the outside it has none. It has nothing to justify it at a universal level'.[4]

Other examples of this impossibility of exchange are cited in economics 'between production and social wealth' and in the media 'between news coverage and real events'.[5] It is when considering the morally complex arena of biology and genetic engineering that Baudrillard points to the fundamental atheism of this contemporary predicament: 'the crucial question is left unanswered: who rules over life, who rules over death?'[6] In a direct allusion to Nietzsche, perhaps the greatest exponent of the atheistic condition, Baudrillard states that 'the values, purposes and causes we delineate are valid only for a form of thought which is human, all too human. They are irrelevant to any other reality whatever (perhaps even to "reality" *tout court*)'.[7]

So there is a fundamental disconnection in hyperreality: between appearances and what lies behind them, between human systems of order and morality and what they seek to differentiate. And all the while, on the surface of things we seek to extend technology and efficiency, eradicating all that goes against the system: death,

negativity, absence. 'Illusion is the fundamental rule'.[8] Baudrillard
frequently seeks to illustrate this with economic language – both
to illustrate that finance itself has become 'mad speculation which
reaches a peak in the virtual economy', and also to illustrate how this
anarchic deregulation to mask the unacceptable is characteristic of
all spheres: 'All current strategies boil down to this: passing around
the debt, the credit, the unreal, unnameable thing you cannot get rid
of'.[9] Baudrillard adopts a Nietzschean reading of Christianity (itself
based on a rather graceless and punitive form of Protestantism) to
argue that this kind of strategy was the 'ruse of God':

> In redeeming man's debt by the sacrifice of His son, God, the
> great Creditor, created a situation where the debt could never
> be redeemed by the debtor, since it has already been redeemed
> by the creditor. In this way, He created the possibility of an
> endless circulation of that debt, which man will bear as his
> perpetual sin.[10]

Exactly the same strategy characterizes the 'ruse of capital', which,
'at the same time as it plunges the world into ever greater debt, works
simultaneously to redeem that debt, thus creating a situation where
it will never be able to be cancelled or exchanged for anything'.[11]

While he is clearly dismissive of Christianity here, Baudrillard
believes that the death of God has not been the liberation of
humanity as Nietzsche hoped, but has placed the futile burden on
human beings to master and transform the world. 'It is only since
God died that the destiny of the world has become our responsibility.
Since it can now no longer be justified in another world, it has to
be justified here and now'.[12] So we strive for an equivalent to the
Kingdom of God, this fanciful eradication of negativity and evil that
is the virtual and the hyper. It is a secular version of redemption and
it is profoundly destructive – of the natural world, of any difference
or otherness, and, ironically, of human freedom. Again, Baudrillard
returns to Mauss' logic of symbolic gift exchange:

> Another explanation for our fall from grace is that the world is
> given to us. Now, what is given we have to be able to give back.
> In the past we could give thanks for the gift, or respond to it by
> sacrifice. Now we have no one to give thanks to. And if we can no
> longer give anything in exchange for the world, it is unacceptable.

So we are going to have to liquidate the given world. To destroy it by substituting an artificial one, built by scratch, a world for which we do not have to account to anyone.[13]

In interpreting this passage, William Pawlett suggests that themes of symbolic debt, counter-gift or potlatch are central to understanding this predicament of impossible exchange and its catastrophic consequences:

We do not want to be indebted to God, who increased our debt by sacrificing his son for us, so we construct an artificial world of signs that is ours. Yet we are now indebted to ourselves, to our reason, our science and our consumer capitalist economy. We can only settle this debt, once for all, by destroying the system, and by destroying ourselves through the construction of virtual reality as the total replacement for humanity and the social world.[14]

The new redemption is virtual reality in all its forms: the digital, universal computation, cloning. This is a gnostic move into the virtual since it is essentially a denial of the physical, the source of decay and mortality. As Rowan Williams has said, 'so far from being a materialist culture, we are a culture that is resentful about material reality, hungry for anything and everything that distances us from the constraints of being a physical animal subject to temporal processes, to uncontrollable changes and to sheer accident'.[15] Aware of the genocidal connotations, Baudrillard describes this move into virtual reality as the 'final solution', a solution for our age where all 'the magical, metaphysical, religious systems which worked in the past are now a dead letter'. It is 'a much more radical solution than all the others . . . since it will no longer have to be exchanged for some transcendence or finality from elsewhere, but for itself, by the substitution of a double which is infinitely 'truer', infinitely more real than the real world . . . An automatic writing of the world in the absence of the world. Total equivalence, total screen, final solution'.[16]

The age of the non-event

This age of virtual reality, of the 'total screen' and of the dominance of media representation is described by Baudrillard as the age of the 'non-event'. In his earlier writing this seems to be informed by the Cold War stalemate and the impasse of mutual nuclear deterrence. The Cold War was a sign of frozen history, the 'end of history', not in Fukuyama's post-Cold War sense of the triumph of capitalism but of a general impossibility of events taking place. Since the fall of the Berlin Wall his understanding of the 'non-event' has been progressively shaped by an understanding of the replacement of reality with media representation: 'We are passing into a realm where events no longer truly take place, by dint of their very production and dissemination in "real time" – where they become lost in the void of news and information'.[17] The non-event is not, therefore, an era when nothing happens. It is more the case that, first, the reality of events is made entirely inaccessible to us by their media codification and, second, the hyperbolic manipulation of events by this representation leaves every event unresolved and unremarkable, simply another commodity circulating in the marketplace of news. The non-event is 'the realm of perpetual change, of a ceaseless updating, of an incessant succession in real time, which produces this general equivalence, this indifference, this banality that characterizes the zero degree of the event'.[18]

Baudrillard regards contemporary warfare as the arena of the hyperreal *par excellence*. War has, he argues, been exchanged 'for the signs of war'.[19] This led to Baudrillard's controversial and most celebrated claim that the Gulf War did not happen. After the 'hot wars' of the early twentieth century and the 'Cold War' that followed, this was 'the dead war – the unfrozen cold war'.[20] This is the war in which 'our virtual has definitively over-taken the actual and we must be content with this extreme virtuality'.[21] Conceived as a hyperreal event, the central meaning of Baudrillard's denial is that the reality of this war was obscured and exhausted by its media coverage, particularly the way in which all possibilities are exhausted in advance as it becomes a manipulated spectacle for consumption: 'The Americans fought the same war in respect of world opinion – via the media, censorship, CNN, etc. – as they fought on the battle-field. They used the same 'fuel air' explosives in the media, where they draw all the oxygen out of public opinion'.[22]

Moreover, in a war where one side has such evident military superiority (characteristic of those wars covered by the Western media), the outcome is so predetermined that the actual events of the war are no longer seen to matter. This also applies to the casualties of the war whom Baudrillard does not deny but views as irrelevant to the way in which the war is presented for consumption. Slavoj Žižek has argued similarly that, rather like decaffeinated-tea and alcohol-free beer, the modern consumer wants war without casualties (on our side at least), 'a virtual war fought behind computer screens, a war experienced by its participants as a video game'.[23]

For Baudrillard, war is a 'non-event' because its simulation through the media is consumed in advance and we consumers are totally dependent on authorities for information about what is going on. This perspective is not, as many have argued, a trivialization of war.[24] Rather, to expose the distortion of reality in this way is a source of resistance, a singularity within the totality. It is to 'give it [war] force in the imagination – somewhere other than in the "real time" of news where it simply peters out. You give force to the illusion of war, rather than become an accessory to its false reality'.[25]

In contrast to the media-driven trivialization of violence, Baudrillard gives much consideration to the presence of violence in the hyperreal. His language (quoted above) of the destruction of the Real makes clear that Baudrillard discerns a violent undercurrent beneath the affluent veneer of consumer culture. Under his Maussian logic, consumerist materialism overwhelms us with its 'gift' and the symbolic debt is frequently repaid through seemingly unaccountable violence. Many have struggled to interpret the motivation behind the riots in London in the summer of 2011, but words written by Baudrillard over 40 years before sound eerily pertinent:

> It is because we base our lives on the traditional idea of the pursuit of well-being as a *rational* activity that the eruptive, unaccountable violence of the Stockholm youth gangs, of the Montreal riots, of the Los Angeles murderers, seems an incredible, incomprehensible manifestation and one which stands in apparent contradiction to social progress and affluence.[26]

He contends that the well-being of consumerist affluence is, in fact, an unnatural anaesthetizing to our natural desire for a more meaningful symbolic exchange. Affluence is 'a system of constraint of a new type' which engenders 'guilt, malaise and profound incompatibilities'. The kind of violence we see in the consumer society is, therefore, 'radically different from the violence engendered by poverty, scarcity and exploitation, [it] is the emergence, in action, of the negativity of desire which is omitted, occulted, censored by the total positivity of need'.[27]

As we saw in the last chapter, symbolic exchange and seduction can take a variety of forms, but there is no doubt that symbolic violence is one of the most prevalent and powerful forms of the counter-gift that Baudrillard perceives in the contemporary world. Violence is the most common challenge to the culture of the perpetual non-event:

> Ruptural events, unforeseeable events, unclassifiable in terms of history, outside of historical reason, events which occur against their own image, against their own simulacrum. Events that break the tedious sequence of current events as relayed by the media, but which are not, for all that, a reappearance of history or a Real interrupting in the heart of the Virtual (as has been said of 11 September). . . They are the internal convulsion of history. And, as a result, they appear inspired by some power of evil, appear no longer to be bearers of a constructive disorder, but of an absolute disorder.[28]

It is in the context of this broader function of symbolic violence that Baudrillard has always theorized about terrorism. True to the structuralist approach, he goes beyond the aims and motivations of the terrorists themselves to ask what signifying effect violent events have within our culture. This topic is addressed in detail in Chapter 6.

Alterity in a whitewashed life

The fable of the Faustian pact with the devil is a recurring theme in Baudrillard's writing. In the conclusion of *The Consumer Society*, he tells the story of the Student of Prague who sold his reflection to the devil to further his romantic ambitions with a rich young woman. But his image begins to appear as a double and haunts him wherever he goes. The double commits crimes that are attributed to him, as if taking revenge for having been sold. Eventually the student tracks down his double and shoots him. But, of course, in killing his shadow he has killed himself.

Although written before his tight formulation of the precession of simulacra, this fable represents much of Baudrillard's core philosophy. In submitting to a total logic of commodification (selling his image to the devil), our culture has created a (potentially malevolent) hyperreal version of itself which has exterminated its original (reality). The subject has been assassinated by its object. 'The object (the soul, the shadow, the product of our labour become object) *takes its revenge*'.[29] In later writings, it is a version of this story in which the man's *shadow* is sold that appeals to Baudrillard, since the shadow represents the darkness, the negativity, the ambivalence of the counter gift, that hyperreality seeks to eradicate:

> Ours is rather like the situation of the man who has lost his shadow: either he has become transparent, and the light passes right through him or, alternatively, he is lit from all angles, overexposed and defenceless against all sources of light. We are similarly exposed on all sides to the glare of technology, images and information, without any way of refracting their rays; and we are doomed in consequence to a whitewashing of all activity – whitewashed social relations, whitewashed bodies, whitewashed memories – in short, to a complete aseptic whiteness. Violence is whitewashed, history is whitewashed, all as part of a vast enterprise of cosmetic surgery at whose completion nothing will be left but a society for which, and individuals for whom, all violence, all negativity, are strictly forbidden.[30]

We should not delude ourselves that this banishing of negativity and violence is to be celebrated since the whitewashing of which Baudrillard speaks is not redemptive cleansing but a rendering totally superficial of all culture and society. In other words, we find ourselves in a world devoid of alterity, of otherness. It is Baudrillard's radical thesis that it is in our endless endeavour to eradicate our world of all that we perceive to be dangerous – illness, risk, hostility, ugliness, criminality – that we have pushed out any potential for engagement with otherness, potential for true, transformative relationship.

This is the supremacy of the Code: a totalized joining together of people and things through a saturation of communication. In the virtual world of simulation, there is the possibility of 'playing at being an Other, pretending, which is not quite the same thing'.[31]

Eventually, 'the great Other would be the code and there would be no Other. . . On the other side of the code, there may be no more Other'.[32] The final chapter of this book takes a closer look at the meaning of alterity in Baudrillard's work from a theological perspective. Here it will suffice to say that the question for a real engagement with otherness – through symbolic exchange, through the fatal, through seduction – remains crucially important to Baudrillard and the theme of how we cultivate relationality will feature in all the subsequent chapters of this book. 'Some have aptly stated that our true journey is the Other or others. In the end, the only voyage is the one made in relation to the Other, be it an individual or a culture'.[33]

Clearly much of what has been set out in Part I of this book reflects a dispiriting state of affairs in the world today to which theologians need to respond. Baudrillard describes a superficial, secularlized world of 'lost icons' (to quote the title of Rowan Williams' book seeking to provide just such a theological response to 'apathy and narcissism in our imaginative world'[34]). Baudrillard provides an ideal resource for this and, if he at times appears extreme in his pessimistic pronouncements, it is worth remembering that his writings from the 1970s and 1980s now read as eerily prophetic, particularly in relation to the significance of terrorism and the impact of virtual reality. But Baudrillard's work is too often viewed as an unmitigated counsel of despair. In fact, it is Baudrillard's contention that what stands outside simulation (symbolic exchange, seduction, evil and so on) continues to permeate these systems. Part II of this book will therefore explore how his eccentric work on these themes provide a fruitful dialogue partner for the theologian seeking to articulate a new language of encounter with the Other – both with the human other and with God – in the whitewashed, hyperreal age.

PART TWO

5

Sacraments and simulacra

Symbolic rituals can absorb anything, including the organless body of capitalism.[1]

There is a curious irony about Jean Baudrillard in relation to religion. Of the twentieth century French Marxist and post-Marxist theorists, he is among those most drawn towards ritualistic themes: sacrifice, symbolic performance, ceremony, meaning generated through shared signs and so on. Yet, while this might lead us to suspect the influence of catholic piety, Baudrillard was from a Protestant family. We may perhaps recognize this Reformed heritage in his suspicion of the Sign and his instinct for iconoclasm, and we should not be surprised that his discussion of Christianity (in contrast to primitive and Eastern religions) often veers towards doctrine rather than practice. But it is nonetheless in the power of the symbol and symbolic ritual that he sees most potential for resistance against the hyperreal. He draws support for this, of course, from pre-modern societies rather than the sacramental life of the Church. This may be attributable to his Protestant background, but it is no doubt also a legacy of Marx's insistence that Christian faith was not a source of liberation for the masses. Rather it exacerbated and sanctified their alienation.

Baudrillard's great influence while working at the University of Nanterre, Henri Lefevre, exemplifies this belief in the oppressive impact of Catholic culture on the French people through history.

In a scathing pseudo-prayer he writes, 'O Church, O Holy Church, when I finally managed to escape from your control I asked myself where your power came from. Now I can see through your sordid secrets. . .Now I can see the fearful depths, the fearful reality of human alienation!'[2] In *Notes Written One Sunday*, Lefebvre describes a visit to a country church where he semiotically reads the church building in his Marxist dialectical method. Mass then begins and he analyses the power structures and alienating signification of the liturgy. For him the eucharistic symbolism is not generative of enlightenment and community but is parodic and superficial. To him the core material symbols of bread and wine are controlled and manipulated by the priest (representative of the bourgeoisie) and the concepts of solidarity and sociality are entirely spiritualized:

> So this is what the holy meal has been reduced to: torn away from community to be accomplished by those who mediate between us and the absolute – torn away from the life of the senses and from real festivity to become symbolic, abstract, distant. Transformed entirely to another plane – a spiritual and 'interior' plane, apparently. But where is the human community for these people in black I see filing back to their seats, their eyes half-closed, their hands clasped piously together, absorbed in the dreariness of what their mouths and their souls have just tasted? A caricature of community! Profound? Inner? No! These dehumanized beings are self-absorbed from the moment they are born to the moment they die, and the only community they know is fictitious and abstract.[3]

It might be said that, in this reading, the mass has taken on the form of the kind of alienating self-referentiality that characterizes the hyperreal. The bread and wine have been cut off from their referent of 'real festivity' and neither does Lefebvre see any evidence among these 'dehumanized beings' that these signs operate sacramentally to connect them with any higher power. They are empty signifiers which create a highly alienating system.

Baudrillard would no doubt share much of this analysis. We saw his contention in Chapter 2 that what has long attracted people to Church is hollow spectacle, the 'immanence of ritual'.[4] Yet we have also seen Baudrillard's interest in the ritual life of primitive societies and particularly Mauss' understanding of symbolic exchange as a source of generating communion and sociality in the face of nihilistic individualism. The rest of this chapter will explore the relevance of Baudrillard's work on ritual to Christian theology, arguing that a Christian understanding of sacramentality has more in common with his conception of symbolic exchange than he seems willing to consider. The discussion of sacramentality and the Eucharist in this chapter should not be seen merely as of narrow interest to liturgists. Baudrillard's consideration of ritual and symbolic exchange as a site of human renewal and 'becoming' adds weight to the growing theological trend to view worship and praise as the proper site of theological insight.[5]

Sign and symbol

In *For a Critique of the Political Economy of the Sign*, Baudrillard sets out a basic distinction between the sign and the symbol, which he then develops extensively in *Symbolic Exchange and Death*. According to Baudrillard, the consumer economy has reduced the processes of signification in a fundamental way. He views consumerism as constructed by the circulation of objects as signs, lacking any kind of singularity and thus no longer objects in which we can have any real interest, investment or committed responsibility. Baudrillard seeks to explain this in the contrast between signs and symbols. He highlights the distinction with the example of a wedding ring. This object is not a sign but a *symbol*; it is the 'concrete manifestation of a total relationship of desire',[6] a singular object. The wedding ring is the shared expression of the commitment, its circularity a reminder of the eternity to which the couple consecrate their relationship. A cosmetic ring, however, is an object of consumption which is a pure sign, gaining its meaning from its signification within the complex determinations of the fashion system.

Baudrillard's contention is that objects generally are drifting towards the status logic of sign value, losing their symbolic value and thus the unitive function they play between individuals. Choice of housing, for example, has traditionally been driven by symbolic motivations with people living in inherited family-built houses, fused with sentimental and relational significance. Increasingly, however, accommodation is becoming a commodity, indexed to social mobility and status: housing as sign. Here Baudrillard echoes the work of Herbert Marcuse, whose theory of 'operationalism' (also driven by marketization) illustrates how 'the progress of technological rationality is liquidating the oppositional and transcending elements in the "higher culture"'.[7]

In reflecting on the meaning and purpose of liturgy, many sacramental theologians have drawn a similar distinction between sign and symbol, as have biblical scholars following Paul Ricoeur's work on the role of metaphor.[8] Signs operate according to a logic of value-exchange and refer to something other than themselves. They are rational and their signification can be learnt intellectually. By contrast, symbols draw us into a more complex relation between persons of which the symbol itself is more than a mere signifier. As such, the symbol is intuitive and touches on the whole realm of feeling and senses. Reflecting on the role of symbols in the creative imagination, Paul Avis draws the distinction that 'Signs serve to remind us of what we already know; symbols speak of things beyond our ken'.[9] While this is generally true (although it is not always the case that we know what signs signify), Avis appears to be drawing on Tillich's reading of the symbol to emphasize our individual *existential* involvement. In Baudrillard's work there is much more of Mauss' sense of the relational and unitive role of symbols. Symbols are about connection. While we may have some loose sense of connection to one another through the common knowledge of what a sign signifies, the symbol actually signifies and mediates our relationality. It is this unitive role of the symbolic and its transcendence of rational exchange that places it at the heart of the liturgical life.

The French sacramental theologian Louis-Marie Chauvet has engaged with both Baudrillard and Mauss in considering how economic logic and consumer desire have given previously meaningful objects a superficiality and transience within the system of consumption. He uses Baudrillard's argument that, in the consumer society, merchandize is immediately produced as sign. Production arises only out of the ideological need that creates it, living from its own reproduction as an encoded sign-value. Chauvet is particularly interested in how symbolic exchange is neutralized by the impossibility, in consumer capitalism, of offering the return gift that is any act of reciprocity. As consumers we are urged to have everything, but we can give nothing back.

Society gratifies us with its gifts and offers us all the 'security' possible so that we may be completely assured of not losing anything from our hoards of valuables by theft, fire, sickness, accident, even beyond death (life insurance). But, at the same time, society snatches away the right to give a return-gift and it is a heavy ransom to pay.[10]

Chauvet appears more optimistic than Baudrillard in maintaining that not every social process has degenerated into sign function. Mauss' system of 'obligatory generosity', organized according to a process of gift→reception→return-gift,[11] continues to pervade our exchanges. Symbols continue to allow us to live as subjects and continue to structure all our relations as mediations of the authentically human. Yet at points, Baudrillard also maintains this priority of symbolic exchange of sign function. In 2003 he wrote that he would be 'quite willing to believe that there has never been any economy in the rational scientific sense in which we understand it, that symbolic exchange has always been the radical base of things, and that it is on that level that things are decided'.[12]

Chauvet ascribes three characteristics to the symbols that pervade our culture. First, the function of the symbol is not, like that of the sign, to refer to a 'something else' that always stands on the plane of value, measure and calculation. The primary function of the symbol is to join the *persons* who produce or receive it within their cultural world (social, religious, economic) and so *to identify them as subjects in their relations with other subjects*. Second, the symbol does not, therefore, provide information *about* the real but information *of* the real. The symbol is not a representation of objects but a communication between subjects. Third, Chauvet explicitly associates the sign with the capitalist economy and the symbol with pre-industrial society: the difference between sign and symbol 'thus appears as *homologous* to the difference which exists between the principle of objective value, which governs the *marketplace*, and the principle 'beyond value' of interpersonal communication, which governs *symbolic exchange*'.[13] Thus the symbol reflects a more profound mode of interpersonal communication that the sign.

Since symbols precede value, key terms in describing them are 'graciousness and gratuitousness'.[14] The sign logic of value is contrasted with the symbolic logic of super-abundance. It is precisely because symbolic exchange occurs in the order of non-value that it is of use 'in thinking through the gratuitous and gracious relation effected between humankind and God in the sacraments'.[15] So

Chauvet develops his response to the sign/symbol dichotomy into an examination of the symbolic exchange at work in the Eucharistic Prayer. He contrasts his symbolic approach with instrumental understandings of the Eucharist which are more frequently associated with a sacrifice of expiation. These are more in danger of adopting the value logic of the sign since a theology of the mass as 'redeeming sacrifice' is more liable to drift towards a mercantile notion of exchange. Here Chauvet follows the philosopher René Girard[16] in viewing the Eucharist as anti-sacrificial. The heart of the Eucharist is *'to convert all that is sacrificial to the Gospel in order to live it out, not as slaves, but as brothers and sisters'.*[17] In this approach Chauvet seeks to reconcile Catholic teaching with Protestant perspectives since a core Reformation polemic was against precisely this reduction of sacraments as mediations of grace to a mercantile exchange system.

Chauvet finds this emphasis on communion accomplished through symbolic exchange as rooted in the reciprocity of the eucharistic offering as conceived in the Roman Catholic Eucharistic Prayer II.[18] It is worth setting out Chauvet's argument here in some detail. The very structure of this Eucharistic Prayer, he argues, mirrors Mauss' structure of Gift→Reception→Return-gift. The presentation of the Christian story in the Prayer of Institution expresses the gift of Jesus Christ to the Church. The recited story of the Last Supper 'effects the Church's acted-out confession of faith, recognising that its existence is dependent on Jesus, its Lord'.[19]

The heart of the sacrament lies in the reception of this gift, which Chauvet locates in the anamnesis discourse. However, the character of this reception is itself in the form of an offering, indicated by the principal verb 'we offer you . . . '. This is the paradox that makes possible the symbolic exchange which consumer capitalism, lacking reciprocity, denies: the reception of the gift of Christ is effected by an oblation.[20] Simultaneously we 'call to mind Christ's death on the cross' and 'we offer . . . this life-giving bread, this saving cup'. God's own grace is rendered back to God.

Following on from this reception, the return-gift of the Church is fundamentally its ethical practice. In the final section of the Eucharistic prayer, the Church begs to become the ecclesial body of Christ through the power of the Spirit. This is the true oblation that the Church offers: 'Members of the assembly are committed to live out their own oblation in self-giving to others, as Christ did, as *fraternal agape*'.[21] Thus the 'giving thanks' of the Eucharist is enfleshed in the living-in-grace among brothers and sisters that is the Body of Christ, the Church. This is the product and experience of symbolic exchange such as Baudrillard and Mauss search for in primitive societies. It overcomes the utility and equivalence of exchange value and allows real relations to emerge in the grace-filled sociality of the Church.

Chauvet's analysis sets out a coherent understanding of how the text of the liturgy expresses a fundamental challenge to the way in which advanced capitalism can destroy meaningful human relations. In so doing, he successfully challenges an atonement theology that works according to a dangerous logic of value exchange and a sacramental theology that unhelpfully isolates the Eucharist from its essential ecclesial identity. However, his analysis remains largely theoretical which precludes any serious discussion of how the semiotics of the rite can form our perception and being in the world. Chauvet's liturgical analysis is essentially text-based, using a profoundly language-based Saussurean semiology: 'It is in language that symbolic exchange, along with the subject, takes its origin'.[22]

The ceremony of the world

Chauvet's analysis of the Eucharistic Prayer illustrates how it can be understood as a symbolic exchange in the way Baudrillard outlines in *Symbolic Exchange and Death*. However, Baudrillard's interest in ritual is grounded in a broader semiotics which he explores further in *Fatal Strategies*, much of which explores his understanding of the 'ceremony of the world' as an unmarketized social practice.[23] I am going to draw out five themes from Baudrillard's exploration of ceremony that are pertinent to Christian liturgical practice and theology more widely.

First, as we have seen above, Baudrillard's interest in ritual is fundamentally as the cultivation of a *social relation*. He is not interested in personal piety or spirituality. This is what lends his work to Chauvet's particularly collective interpretation of Eucharistic presence.[24] Given the fundamental reciprocity and connectedness involved, Baudrillard views symbolic exchange as something that undermines the very 'reality principle' of modernity which he believes to be essentially atomizing and fragmenting. Scientific rationalism and the constructs of modern understanding have dismembered things that should be seen as more closely interrelated. In contrast, ceremony reverses modernity's structural divisions of life and death, natural and cultural, body and soul:

> The symbolic is neither a concept, an agency, a category, nor a 'structure', but an act of exchange and *a social relation which puts an end to the real*, which resolves the real, and, at the same time, puts an end to the opposition between the real and imaginary... The symbolic is what puts an end to this disjunctive code and to separated terms. *It is the u-topia that puts an end to the topologies of the soul and the body, man and nature, the real and the non-real, birth and death.* In symbolic operation, the two terms lose their reality.[25]

Second, as much of *Symbolic Exchange and Death* seeks to demonstrate, the overcoming of this modern binarism is rooted in an overturning of modernity's denial of death. We saw in Chapter 3 Baudrillard's exploration of the way in which primitive initiation rites come to a new accommodation with death. Consistent with his view of the Church as a repressive force that seeks to control death (and hence life) rather than engage with it symbolically, he emphatically rejects the strong resonances that this ceremony has with the Christian ceremony of Baptism.[26] This seems unfortunate and unwarranted since baptism is quite conventionally understood as a death to self in order to bring about birth into the community of the Church. St Paul's Letter to the Romans expresses this idea: 'Therefore we have been buried with Him through baptism into death, so that as Christ was raised from the dead through the glory of the Father, so we too might walk in newness of life'.[27] There seem to be strong parallels here with Baudrillard's thought in terms of the death of the individual ego and a new openness to collectivity and communion.

Similar themes emerge again in *Fatal Strategies* where ceremony is seen as ending the 'occultism of subjectivity'.[28] Here collective ritual seems to lend itself to a positive understanding of the death of the subject (discussed further in Chapter 10). Baudrillard sees this relativizing of subjectivity partly in the regulative dimension of religious ritual practice. He quotes extensively from the Hindu Code of Manu which is similar to the Book of Leviticus from the Hebrew Scriptures in its detailed ritualizing of domestic and personal life: 'every moment marked with a necessary sign'.[29] Baudrillard seems drawn to the idea of ceremony, therefore, as a submission to something higher than subjective human will. 'This is where signs take on their greatest intensity: when they require only pure observance'.[30] Ritual practice is seen as incongruous by the modern world, insufficiently 'customer-oriented' and pointlessly repetitive in an age when people seek to maximize experience. But Baudrillard sees this challenging of the logic of consumer choice as precisely its attraction and power:

> All of this might seem to us, in the moral, sentimental and democratic order in which we live, perfectly immoral and unjustifiable; in fact, we have long directed our fulminations at predestination and discrimination, while we cultivate lovingly, on the contrary, finality and difference – however it is in predestination and discrimination that things and signs attain their highest level of intensity, fascination and *jouissance*.[31]

Third, ceremony represents for Baudrillard a kind of fluidity of identity and *interchangeability of form*. In bringing about the death of subjectivity and an intensity of social relations, symbolic exchange seems to permit a broad sense of transubstantiation that takes us beyond the interpersonal:

> So the animal form, the human form, the divine form are exchanged according to the rule of metamorphoses in which each ceases to be confined to its definition, with the human opposed to the inhuman, etc. There is a symbolic circulation of things in which none has a separate individuality, in which all operate in a kind of universal collusiveness of inseparable forms.[32]

In other words, ceremony brings into operation a new system of representation. The binary relationship between sign and signifier is replaced by a more complex drawing together of things in symbolic signification. There is a parallel here to Foucault's theory of resemblances[33] where signification operates through chains of multiple connotations rather than straightforward binary denotation. Christian liturgy also plays with this interchangeability of animal, human and divine forms. The bread and wine represent

Jesus, who is described as the Lamb of God. But the bread and wine also represent the people, the Church, who are themselves described as the body of Christ. Attempts to fix form and identity within ceremony lead to an inevitable reduction in meaning. Resistance to this kind of reduction is the fourth theme of Baudrillard's conception of ceremony. Ritual plays the essential role of *resisting functionality* and over-determinism. Ceremony is subversive of the 'norms of reality' and should be seen, in this sense, as potentially reckless and risky. Here Baudrillard paradoxically holds in tension the sense in which ceremony is regulative (as we saw above), a 'perfect ordering'[34] of the world, and the sense in which this is achieved through the overturning of the order of logic and rationality in favour of perceived disorder and chaos. Perversely it is the over-organization of the world through science and managerialism that is eroding the deeper symbolic order:

The world will end – literally – when all seductive rapports yield to rational ones. This is precisely the catastrophic enterprise on which we are engaged: resolving all fatality into causality or probability. That is true entropy.[35]

The risk involved in abandoning the securities of causality and reason through participation in ceremony leads Baudrillard to compare ritual with gambling, a game regulated by rules rather than an operation regulated by law. It is this replacement of certainty with chance that 'allows the arbitrary modality of the game (concrete rules) for ceremonial purposes (and not for contractual purposes, as in exchanges regulated by law), as a perfectly conventional ritual where there is reflected – not without a glimmer of irony – the absolute necessity that underlies hope'. And this is ceremony's attraction, that it offers us hope by freeing us from the determinism of certainty and law. After all, Baudrillard suggests, 'we are all gamblers. What we most intensely desire is that the inexorable procession of rational connections cease for a while'.[36] This is part of the destabilizing function of liturgy that it opens up new possibilities for change in our lives by encouraging us to take risks as acts of faith.

Finally, Baudrillard's understanding of ceremony has a kind of *eschatological dimension* to it. The way in which Baudrillard challenges the linear understanding of time and his understanding of potential for singularity within time will be explored in Chapter 6. But here it will suffice to say that he rejects a meaningful historical narrative: 'ceremony has no meaning, it has only esoteric rule. It has no end, since it is initiatory'.[37] However, ceremony permits a rediscovering of meaningful conjunctions that he chooses to call *destiny*, 'an ineluctable and recurrent unfolding of signs and appearances – has become for us a strange and unacceptable form. We no longer want a destiny. We want a history. But ceremony was the image of destiny'.[38] We will return to the theme of destiny in Chapter 6.

Sacramental singularities

Symbolic ritual has the potential, therefore, to rehabilitate some kind of communion within the flotation of signs that is Baudrillard's hyperreality. It can generate singularity within the system of empty signifiers. We see this kind of idea in Jean-Luc Marion's account of the sacrament or icon, particularly in his essay *The Blind at Shiloh*.[39] Marion accepts Baudrillard's views of a society reduced to simulated spectacle. Images have been emancipated to the point where 'the world is made into an image . . . we live in the audiovisual epoch of history'.[40] Furthermore, like Baudrillard's simulacra, it is an image that is cut off from its original: a signifier without a signified. In a society which Baudrillard has described as 'screened out',[41] images no longer have any other reality than the image itself. Here we see parallels with Baudrillard's political culture of the non-event:

> An event does not prove its reality by having indeed taken place; for if it takes place, it takes place only in a determinate time and place, with actors and spectators in a limited number, in short in a world that is defined since it is real. And yet the real world has disappeared, since the image there makes a screen of its counter-world; henceforth, to have actually taken place, the event must be produced in the counter-world itself.[42]

Marion shares Baudrillard's pessimism about the loss of both sociality and human agency since the 'onanism of the gaze'[43] that this visual culture propagates goes against all forms of communion. In response, therefore, Marion looks for the 'images that give' or 'icons'. The depiction of a figure looking out at the viewer is a fundamental attribute of the traditional icons of the Orthodox Churches. Yet here he is expanding the category of the icon to any image which 'envisages me'. 'It is a matter not so much of seeing a spectacle as of seeing another gaze that sustains mine, confronts it, and eventually overwhelms it'.[44] For Marion the paradigm of iconicity is Jesus Christ who offers 'not only a visible image of the Father who remains invisible but even a (visible) face of the invisible itself (the Father), a visible image of the invisible *as invisible*'.[45]

Marion is reluctant to define exactly where this iconicity is experienced. He puts great importance on loving face-to-face contact between human beings. But beyond this, in the uncertainty of contemporary culture, the possible origin of other such liberating icons remains unknown. However, for Marion, it is in the liturgy that 'the paradigmatic kenosis of the image for the benefit of the holiness of God'[46] is accomplished:

> The liturgy alone impoverishes the image enough to wrest it [our gaze] from every spectacle, so that in this way might appear the splendor that the eyes can neither hope for nor bear, but a splendor that love – shed abroad in our hearts [Romans 5.5] – makes it possible to endure.[47]

Marion sees liturgical symbols or sacraments as 'saturate signs' or 'signs of abundance'. At times, Baudrillard presents his understanding of the singularity of the complete opposite. For him the uniqueness of the sign lies in the fact that it is 'a sign without content'.[48] This expresses his conviction that 'rational signification' within the system of signs is what has exhausted us and created an excess of superficial meaning. What we dream of are 'senseless events which will free us from this tyranny of meaning'.[49] Liturgy, too, might be understood in this way, a liberation from the 'occultism of subjectivity' described above. But others may see this contrast as the core difference between theologians like Marion and Chauvet and an atheist philosopher like Baudrillard. Marion looks for the 'saturated sign' while Baudrillard sees hope only in the empty, nihilistic sign.

But one of the core arguments of this book is that Baudrillard's nihilism frequently takes on an apophatic character that makes room for a new kind of believing, a new kind of excess. In *Fatal Strategies* he does refer to the excess of the signifier:

> . . . the idea that the signifier is there from the beginning, spread everywhere, in a profusion that happily the signified never exhausts. This overabundant order of the signifier is that of magic (and poetry). It is not an order of chance or indetermination; far from that, it is rather an arranged order, a necessity superior to the one which joins the signifier and the signified [the arbitrary work of reason].[50]

This singularity that is other than reason and logic is the antithesis of capitalism since it is 'that which is impossible to exchange, the portion irreducible to any equivalent whatever'.[51] Thus it is rooted in the concepts Baudrillard associates with ceremony and ritual which is an alternative way of human relating: symbolic exchange, potlatch, gift, interchangeability, destiny. It is these qualities that allow the singularity to be transformative, to make it the site of 'integral becoming', the process of becoming 'what one is not'.[52]

6

Eschatology, terrorism and death

The world is not sufficiently coherent to lead to the Apocalypse.[1]

In his earlier work, Baudrillard's mourning for the loss of death in Western Society is related to the way in which death is central to the symbolic exchange of primitive societies. When we lose the powerful social significance of death we lose a core element in the generation of meaningful human community. But in later writings, this theme explores the way in which death has been lost as a symbolic mediation of all finality. His theory of the loss of subjectivity in the contemporary world is described not so much in terms of the *death* of the self as its *extermination*. He points out that 'to *exterminate* means to deprive something of its own end, to deprive it of its term. It is to eliminate duality, the antagonism of life and death, to reduce everything to a kind of single principle ... of the world which could be said to express itself in all our technologies, particularly today our virtual technologies'.[2] This chapter will explore Baudrillard's writing about time and finality, looking at how the theme of eschatology relates to his important work on terrorism. We will then look briefly at Baudrillard's more 'realized' eschatology in the concept of the singularity, relating it to the New Testament theme of *kairòs*.

The illusion of the end

For Baudrillard, the replacement of death with extermination is not just a matter of individual human lives, it is the state in which our whole civilization finds itself. Perhaps the most important question running through his later work is to ask what it means for a society to have given up on teleology or eschatology. 'The problem raised by history is not that it might have come to an end, as Fukuyama says, but rather that it will have no end – and hence no longer any finality, any purpose'.[3] Baudrillard contends that there is no sense in our world today that we are 'going anywhere' since we lack a conception of history as a narrative ending in culmination, be that annihilation or consummation. 'For us', he writes, 'the mirror of history, the continuity of history is shattered; we live in an instant and disincarnate currentness'.[4]

This has enormous theological implications since the idea of time as a meaningful linear journey that will reach some kind of endpoint is a central concept in the Abrahamic Faiths. The historical narrative began at Creation and will terminate at the Last Judgement. Following the kind of historically grounded teleological philosophies of Hegel and Marx, much twentieth-century theology sought to interpret the Biblical narrative as an interpretation of the meaning of history. G. E. Wright exemplifies this endeavour:

> The Bible is the record of God's acts of wrath, love and salvation in a certain specific history which is set within the framework of all history and presents to all history the hope and certainty of its redemption. The Biblical perspective of time thus carries back before Abraham to the creation. It leads forward to the death and resurrection of Jesus Christ as its mid-point, and beyond that to the end of present history and the dawn of eternity.[5]

As we shall see, Baudrillard does not regret the decline of this kind of eschatological narrative. However, the kind of society he describes under late consumer capitalism is one that has gone to the opposite extreme and lost all sense of meaningful historical narrative. Because of its origins and ethic, Baudrillard again sees America as leading the way here since it was 'created in the hope of escaping from history, of building a utopia sheltered from history, and ... it has in part succeeded in that project, a project that it is still pursuing today'.[6] America is a society that has founded itself, not on a process of historical evolution as might be said of the European nations, but on a set of philosophical utopian principles. Thus it undervalues both past and future in its fixation with a fantastic utopian present. 'Having known no primitive accumulation of time, it lives in a perpetual present. Having seen no slow, centuries-long accumulation of the principle of truth, it lives in perpetual simulation, in a perpetual present of signs'.[7]

But the dominance of immediate visual culture, a preoccupation with the superficial interplay of signs is coming to characterize life in all advanced capitalist societies. So everywhere we are seeing the disintegration of linear time narratives as a result of a three-fold process. The first process is one of *temporal acceleration*. There is an impatient immediacy about our society; objects, information and images are all circulating at such a speed that all events are pre-empted, reduced to spectacle with predetermined outcomes. In Baudrillard's most famous example, this reduction of events to signs has been exemplified in modern warfare where the outcome is already so predetermined and hyper-anticipated that the conflict itself might be said not to have taken place at all (Chapter 4).[8]

This speed of events has made the whole enterprise of historical reflection an impossibility since history requires a 'degree of slowness', a certain distance to permit 'the kind of condensation or significant crystallization of events we call history, the kind of coherent unfolding of causes and effects we call reality'.[9] In the liberation of events from meaningful sequences (however constructed these were in the past), the possibility of 're-telling' events as an historical narrative on which we can reflect is lost. The advent of 24 hour news channels has provided us with the new experience of being constantly bombarded with information about events as they take place, but without the possibility of critical reflection. A consequence of this is a generalized sense of urgency and alert. Since news items cannot be ranked within a delimited news programme, whatever we are presented with at any given moment is considered to be of singular importance, accompanied by eye-catching printed headlines on the screen underlining its urgency. In the commodification of information, every news item has the status of an immediate crisis to catch our attention. It seems that when we lose eschatology and the idea that history as a whole is heading towards some kind of crisis (for good or ill) we live in a permanent sense of crisis in the present. However, in addition to this process of the speeding up of time, Baudrillard argues that there is also a certain *slowing down*. Just as physics has demonstrated that the density of matter can slow the passing of time, so history is reaching a kind of inertia as it rubs against the 'silent majorities' of the consumer public. At the height of the mobilization and liberation of the masses, we have been hit by 'an equivalent force of inertia, of an immense indifference and the silent potency of that indifference'.[10] This is why Baudrillard pours scorn on Francis Fukuyama's triumphalist declaration of the 'end of history'.[11] History has not come to any sort of conclusion; it is simply not possible to perceive it in a coherent form. It is as if events merely cancel themselves out in a state of indifference. There is no shortage of 'things happening' by which history ought to constitute itself. There is certainly no shortage of violence, which seems to have been Fukayamma's naïve basis for thinking that history was over. Baudrillard is surely correct in stating, 'there will always be more violence'.[12] So what we lack, rather, is the ability to draw meaningful threads between events. We might say that history is accelerating, but the meaning of history is grinding to a halt.

But Baudrillard goes a step further. The loss of teleology has not only resulted in both the speeding up and slowing down of time; history has, in effect, gone into *reverse*. As the millennium approached, Baudrillard reflected that we were trapped in a retroactive process of reliving the twentieth century even while its events had lost significance and meaning for us. This supposed turning point in linear history was marked, not by a looking to the future, but by processes of 'restoration, regression, rehabilitation, revival of old frontiers, of the old differences, of particularities, of religions – and even resipiscence in the sphere of morals'.[13] Since Baudrillard identifies this point of history's reversal as the 1980s we can assume that the religious revival he refers to is both the resurgence of Roman Catholicism in former Soviet bloc countries and the resurgence of a more overt Islamic identity through the Middle East following the Iranian Revolution of 1979. Post-secular theorists might view such trends as resulting from the paucity of secular liberal culture and its values. These movements are certainly testimony to the ability of religious narrative to unite and galvanize people in the face of consumerist individualism. But Baudrillard refuses to be so optimistic, more inclined to view an increased religious fundamentalism as an attempt to 'elude our own deaths'[14] or as an 'enthusiastic work of mourning'.[15] We should certainly recognize an element of this regressive kind of reversal of history in the rise of theological and liturgical conservatism in recent years. Unable to cope with the challenges of a complex and profoundly secularized society, many seek solace in idealized, nostalgic abstractions of religious identity and have sought to undo reforms that are perceived to have compromised authentic faith.

But it is not only religion where Baudrillard identifies a reversal of modern thought. We might say that the postmodern is the playing out of parodic revivals of the modern in all spheres including fashion, art, politics and religion. Thus, Baudrillard suggests, it can hardly be said that history has ended or is, in any real sense, moving forward. He paints a characteristically bleak picture of a society that can embrace neither progress nor death:

> Thus, when we speak of the 'end of history', the 'end of the political', the 'end of the social', the 'end of ideologies', none of this is true. The worst of it all is precisely that there will be no end to anything, and all these things will continue to unfold slowly, tediously, recurrently, in that hysteresis of everything which, like nails and hair, continues to grow after death.[16]

To summarize, all three of these temporal distortions (history's acceleration, its deceleration and its reversal) are manifestations of the 'illusion of the end' under which we are presently living. We live in a society without end or purpose, living through a succession of events we are unable to connect into a meaningful narrative: '[History] is no longer able to transcend itself, to envisage its own finality, to dream of its own end; it is being buried beneath its own immediate effect, worn out in special effects, imploding into current events'.[17]

Taking charge of death

In the context of this 'society without finality', Baudrillard contends that we have taken in certain myths about the possibilities of immortality. They are fanciful myths because immortality can only be conceived in relation to God: 'as soon as that [divinely ordained] order begins to break up, as soon as that transcendence is lost, the cosmic order, like the human order, emancipated from God and all finality, because shifting and unstable . . . The problem of the end becomes crucial and insoluble'.[18] Since the loss of death as a sense of finality in God, we are seeing the transcribing of immortality 'into its technical operation, a transcription of the human race itself into an immortal, artificial species, ensuring its genetic and generic survival by all available means'.[19] As an example of this, Baudrillard reflects a great deal on the phenomena of the cryogenic freezing of terminally ill people who have paid vast amounts of money in the hope of 'cheating death', being revived at a future point in history when they can be cured. This is certainly an unprecedented human defiance of the inevitability of death and of the finality of the human self. In refusing their own deaths, the cryogenically frozen have forfeited all their symbolic significance and consequently, Baudrillard would argue, their own humanity. They have 'wired themselves up' to the network, the matrix, as mere units of information. They have become fully digital:

> These generations . . . no longer expect anything from some future 'coming', and have less and less confidence in history, which dig in behind their futuristic technologies, behind their stores of information and inside the beehive network of communication where time is at last wiped out by pure circulation, will perhaps never reawaken. But they do not know that.[20]

Crucially for Baudrillard, in adopting this digital identity, the cryogenically frozen person takes individualism to a new extreme, since he conserves his existence outside of any reference to the social. Who can say what kind of society he might be reawakened into? But this is of no concern; the survival of a non-social self is taken as sovereign. So cryogenic freezing links together the denial of finality in the individual human and the denial of the very notion of the social. Denial of death is a denial of society since it reflects the abandonment of teleology and the shared experience of time that forms a meaningful narrative in people's lives. In Baudrillard's words, 'The "social" begins by taking charge of death'.[21]

So the question arises of how we reclaim meaning both individually and collectively in a society that lives in a perpetual present condemned to repeat the past. How do we 'take charge of death'? As noted above, Baudrillard does not lament the demise of linear time since this quantification of time was itself a simulation, equally alien to the kind of symbolic societies for which he is nostalgic. In such ritual societies, 'the end of everything is in its beginning and ceremony retraces the perfection of that original event. In contrast to this *fulfilled* order of time, the liberation of the 'real' time of history, the production of a linear, deferred time may seem a purely artificial process'.[22]

Baudrillard sees this structure of linear historical time as having been imposed on Western culture by the Judeo-Christian insistence on Last Judgement and the historical perspective to salvation. But this linear historical perspective is far from the whole story. The Bible also narrates perfection as its original event in the Garden of Eden and the emergence of linear time and finality as a result of its temporary loss. Certainly, the Christian view of history looks to a culmination of time in the creation of a new heaven and a new earth as the final resolution of this problem of temporality, decay and finality.[23] But the Christ event has also put a new perspective on this predicament. Christianity teaches that amidst decay there can be growth, amidst death there can be life and amidst temporality we can find the eternal that was God's original gift in Eden. Baudrillard shows no awareness of this kind of Christian 'realized eschatology'. But his perception of the dangers of a purely futurist eschatology is astute and pertinent to our age. It is these that we explore now before concluding this chapter with an examination of the realized eschatology latent in his concept of the 'singularity'.

Baudrillard argues that all heresies have, in some form or other, taken up this leitmotif of the immediate fulfilment of the promise, which was akin to 'a defiance of time'.[24] If he is slightly too simplistic in his definition of heresy, Baudrillard is right to identify the recurrent temptation to 'cheat God' or 'force his hand' by overcoming history and putting an end to time right away. With the collapse of the linear narrative of history, Baudrillard sees this 'millenarian heresy' as still very present in our society today 'the burning issue remains: "to wait or not to wait?"'[25] This is evidenced in the persistent popularity of millenarian movements and literature, not least the current publishing phenomena of LaHaye and Jenkin's apocalyptic re-telling of current affairs in the 'Left-Behind' series.[26] In these books current events are interpreted as fulfilling the prophecies of the Book of Revelation and the 'rapture' of believers. Such literature has appealed to the American Christian public of whom, according to a poll in 2010, 41% believe that Jesus Christ will return to earth before 2050.[27]

Startlingly, Baudrillard sees this kind of thinking as the definition of 'terrorism', a kind of seductive suicide: 'what, indeed, is terrorism, if not this effort to conjure up, in its own way, the end of history? It attempts to entrap the powers that be by an immediate and total act'.[28] Consequently, contemptuous as right-wing Christians LaHaye and Jenkins would find the accusation, their objectives are not dissimilar to many religiously motivated terrorists we see in the contemporary world. It is the desire to provoke a catastrophe as a 'shortcut' to some sort of resolution, an impatience with history prompted by the feeling that history is going nowhere. For both LaHaye and Jenkins and many contemporary Islamist terrorists, this impatience is with a world that is increasingly hostile to their particularistic notions of religion and cultural identity.[29] In both cases, Baudrillard shows how the loss of a theological teleology is a major source of unrest and anxiety in contemporary society.

Baudrillard dislikes what he understands to be the 'Platonic-Christian' doctrine of the immortality of the soul, viewing it as the Church's means of exerting control over both life and death. But many Christian theologians would argue that the Platonic doctrine of the immortality of the soul (and its subsequent Christianizing by Origen) never was an adequately Christian understanding of the possibilities of eternal life through Christ, and has contributed precisely to the fantasies of atemporality that characterize our age. Origen's belief that the physical embodiment of the soul is merely a phase of purification before returning it to its original spiritual state[30] denigrates corporeal, temporal existence and has been seen by subsequent theologians as inconsistent with belief in Christ's material incarnation. Thus there is a closer connection between the 'heresy of impatience' that Baudrillard identifies and a more general failure of much of the Christian tradition to understand the possibility of immortality as grounded in the restored relationship of soul *and body* with the Creator. Nonetheless, this denigration of physical, temporal life is now even further compounded by the abandonment of belief in life after death of any kind. The rejection of immortality and history go hand in hand. 'What we want is the immediate realization of immortality by all possible means . . . without having resolved the problem of the end . . . This is precisely our fantasy of stepping beyond the end, of emancipating ourselves from time'.[31]

How we seek to 'step beyond the end' varies. Most of us, following the psychological eradication of death, have succumbed to some scientific version of immortality. This may not be the extremes of the cryogenic freezing discussed above, but an overinflated belief in the possibilities of science and medicine is quite widespread. The advent of stem cell research with its regenerative potentials for the human body has renewed discussion about the indefinite deferral of death. This is perhaps a classic example of the reduction of the symbolic into the functional digitality. As Baudrillard describes: 'No more transfiguration, no more metaphors: immortality has passed over into the (biological, genetic) code'.[32]

Increasingly in our age, however, we are seeing attempts to step outside of time and consummate history that are essentially terroristic, exhibiting, 'a demand for a violent resolution of reality, when it eludes our grasp in an endless hyperreality'.[33] This is the radical reintroduction of death as a symbolic quality into a society that denies finality. Baudrillard argues that under advanced capitalism we live under a slow systemic death. After all, in the finite logic of exchange value the equivalence of wages and labour power presupposes the death of the worker. The symbolic can only therefore be cast in the form of some kind of violent death: 'Violent death changes everything, slow death changes nothing, for there is a rhythm, a scansion necessary to symbolic exchange'.[34] It is here that Baudrillard hits upon extremely problematic territory in defining exactly what kind of strategy he is advocating. Using Mauss' logic of symbolic gift exchange (which is short-circuited in the digital society), he defines his strategy thus:

> To defy the system with a gift to which it cannot respond save by its own collapse and death. Nothing, not even the system, can avoid the symbolic obligation, and it is in this trap that the only chance of a catastrophe for capital remains . . . The system must itself commit suicide in response to the multiplied challenge of death and suicide.[35]

Baudrillard emphatically states 'There is no question here of real violence or force'.[36] However, he could not have realized when writing in 1976 how prophetic his theory would appear at the start of the twenty-first century and how effective, spectacular acts of suicidal terrorism appear to be as a challenge (the challenge?) to the advanced capitalist system in the mass-media age. In commenting on the attack on the World Trade Centre in 2001, Baudrillard agrees with the popular liberal view that Islamist terrorists are responding to the humiliation inflicted on marginalized cultures by the West whose mission is 'to subject the many different cultures, by any means available, to the unforgiving law of equivalence'.[37] However, he also insists that we are all subject to this humiliation under a system which denies the possibility of symbolic reciprocity:

> It is not a question, therefore, of a 'clash of civilisations', but of an – almost anthropological – confrontation between an undifferentiated universal culture and everything which, in any field whatever, retains something of an irreducible alterity.[38]

Thus Baudrillard suggests how false is the myth on which political leaders claim so much power that terrorism is ultimately an external force. Terrorism (in its literally or metaphorically violent forms) is the inevitable attempt at a 'counter-gift' within a system of power that strips all of us of our symbolic existence and consigns us all 'to an integral technology, to a crushing virtual reality, to the grip of networks and programmes'.[39] Terrorists on 11th September 2001 sought, in a horrific way, to reopen the symbolic. Perhaps this is why so many commentators remarked that this event felt like 'the re-beginning' of history after the Cold War. In any case, if Baudrillard has correctly discerned something of the elemental quality of terrorism as an expression of the 'impossible exchange' of the hyperreal, then no kind of 'War on Terror', however determinedly waged, can eradicate it. Instead, far more fundamental questions will need to be asked about the modes of exchange and self expression within the dominant forms of social order. Such a shift in policy could only begin with a considered appraisal of Baudrillard's view that terrorism is 'the verdict this society passes on itself, its self-condemnation'.[40]

In his later writing Baudrillard again appropriates Mauss' language to view the problem of terrorism as a confrontation between opposing forms of potlatch. He views the hegemonic system of globalization as its own kind of potlatch, the voracious stripping of all value and particularity which the terroristic potlatch of death seeks to defy. 'The terrorists' potlatch against the West is their own death. Our potlatch is indignity, immodesty, obscenity, degradation and abjection'.[41] Here his description of the Western process of globalization employs language evocative of secularization and desecration, even of developing world critiques of Western religious decline. 'Our truth is always on the side of the unveiling, desublimation, reductive analysis – the truth of the repressed – exhibition, avowal, nudity – nothing is true unless it is desecrated, objectified, stripped of its aura, or dragged onstage'.[42]

So how can we reopen the symbolic and 'take charge of death' in our own lives in a non-terroristic way? For a Christian to argue that we should challenge the 'slow death' of capitalism, which Baudrillard abhors, is to argue that death must be cultivated towards a more self-giving purpose and here Baudrillard would appear to be in agreement. True living is indeed sacrificial. He argues that, 'Against every pious and "revolutionary" of the "Labour (or culture) is the opposite of life" type, we must maintain that the only alternative to Labour is not free time, or non-labour, it is sacrifice'.[43] However, Baudrillard fails to make the fundamental distinction between a life and death given as a *symbolic act of violence* and a life and death given as a *symbolic act of sacrifice*. This distinction is often lost today in the discussion of 'suicide-bombings' where the label of martyrdom is frequently claimed. Christian martyrdom, however, has always been seen as a participation in the sacrificial death of Christ which was not (as with the suicide bomber) an act of violence perpetrated against others, but a supreme act of self-giving to others. True martyrdom is not a desire to bring about a finality and hasten the end. Indeed in its true sense the death of a martyr is not itself the witness but the culmination and final expression of the living witness. In the Book of Acts, the first martyr, Stephen, was stoned as a result of the way he lived his life: 'full of grace and power, doing great wonders and signs among the people'.[44] Stephen did not pursue death but his vocational imitation of Christ led him to this martyrdom. The suicide bomber is a terrorist and not a martyr because it is his or her death itself that constitutes the violent witnessing spectacle; his or her death is not the culmination of a sacrificial life.

Realized eschatology: Singularity and *kairòs*

Baudrillard's work on terrorism points to the dangers of the religious zealot's desire to participate in an inaugurated eschatology (martyring yourself in the hope of hastening some kind of end). But there is also a realized eschatology present in his work (a sense of the presence of alterity in the everyday and the occurrence of significant moments). Baudrillard's category of the *singularity* presents other ways of thinking about how time can be shaped meaningfully in the face of the reductionism of simulation. Singularity allows for a radical alterity that is necessary to generate meaningful periods of time and overturn what he calls 'the event strike'.[45] This need not be an act of terrorism. Indeed he describes the predicament itself as a terror:

> We live in a virtually banalized, neutralized world where, because of a kind of preventive terror, nothing can take place any longer. Therefore everything that breaks through is an event. The definition of an event is not to be unpredictable but to be predestined. It is an irrepressible movement: at one moment, it comes out, and we see the resurgence of everything that was plotted by the Good. It makes a break, it creates an event. It can be on the order of thought or of history. It may take place in art.[46]

Clearly the radical alterity involved in the creation of a singularity is not one that Baudrillard would describe in traditional theological terms. However, his use of the word 'predestined' in this passage is interesting. Elsewhere he describes predestination as the fitting together of things in a particular way: 'such a moment is predestined for a particular other, such a word for another one, as in a poem where you have the impression that the words were always pre-ordained to meet'.[47] So here Baudrillard moves singularity away from the violent and sees it in the poetic, a theme we will return to in Chapter 9. He also identifies singularities as possible in 'language, art, the body or culture'.[48]

We have already explored how liturgy might function to re-enchant signs into a new experience of symbolic exchange. The reshaping of time through singularity functions in a similar way, turning the meaningless passing of time (sign) into what Baudrillard calls 'destiny' (symbol) which is also intrinsically bound up with some kind of meaningful exchange:

> . . . there is an exchange, a dual form, not – contrary to the widespread conception – an individual destiny. Destiny is this symbolic exchange between us and the world, which thinks us and which we think, where this collision and collusion take place, this telescoping of, and complicity between, things.[49]

Understanding singularity as a moment of complicity between things implies some kind of providential conjunction of events. According to this definition, singularity has much in common with the New Testament usage of the word *kairòs*. *Kairòs* is often translated as the 'right time' or 'opportune time' and it indicates a period of intense awareness. *Kairòs* is often used in the New Testament to designate times of prayer[50] and at the beginning of Mark's Gospel, it is the 'time' when Jesus' Kingdom is near. At its fundamental level, therefore, *kairòs* is the time when connections are established, between humanity and God and between humans; it is also a time of symbolic exchange. *Kairòs* is not a term used by Baudrillard but it is found in the work of the Italian Marxist philosopher Antonio Negri whose usage is very similar to Baudrillard's singularity. Negri argues that the connection made possible by *kairòs* is the connection between the signifier and the signified, the fundamental connection that Baudrillard believes to have been lost in the consumer age. *Kairòs* is what makes language and meaning possible. Consequently, it is the time that makes all human relating possible.

Baudrillard's description of the singularity implies that it is very momentary and fragmentary. But Negri (more optimistic generally about political renewal) suggests that singularities accumulate into a meaningful pattern that renews language and relationship:

> *Kairòs* means singularity. But singularities are multiple. So, before a singularity there is always another singularity, and *kairòs* is, so to speak, multiplied in other *kairòs*. When the name is said and heard, each lives in language, every *kairòs* will be open to another *kairòs* – and all together these events of naming will come up in facing one another, in dialogue and perhaps clashing,

constitute common names. It is in relation to alterity that the name spills into the common. Here, being reveals itself as *mit-Sein*, as 'being-with'.[51]

In Baudrillard's account of singularity and in its parallels in Negri's writings, we can see deep resonances with the New Testament theme of *kairòs* and the way in which it is linked with the themes of connection and solidarity. In the Letter to the Ephesians in particular, God's plan in Christ is disclosed as the 'gathering up of all things' (1.10). In creating a new humanity, God has brought Jew and Gentile into a symbolic exchange, reconciling them in one body through the power of Christ's death on the Cross (2.16). Indeed it might be said that much of St Paul's writing is concerned with the generation of singularities that open people's perceptions the symbolic exchange that God is generating among them through the Spirit, forming them into the Body of Christ. Baudrillard gives us a language to think about that in our own age where the mission of the Church is to generate such connection in the face of atomization. Baudrillard challenges us to think what kind of shaping of time enables us to create 'something that leaves a trace in the monotony of the global order of terror. Something that reintroduces a form of impossible exchange in this generalised exchange. Hegemony is only broken by this kind of event, by anything that irrupts as an unexchangeable singularity'.[52]

7

Beyond good and evil

Under the hegemony of good, everything is getting better and, at the same time, going from bad to worse.[1]

Nothing makes the religious thinker more suspicious of postmodern thought than the fear that it masks moral relativism. In its fluid interpretations of the world and the human activity within it, nothing can be judged on absolute terms, and so, the charge goes, no value or action can be considered as 'better' or 'worse' than any other. Good and evil are not seen as having any source or potency of their own. On a superficial reading, Baudrillard appears to fit this nihilistic stereotype entirely. 'Evil', he writes, 'has no objective reality'.[2] Much of his writing is free of any sort of value judgement, adopting a dispassionate, observational style that is alien to the theologian who more often narrates the world within a stable moral universe. But engaging with Baudrillard's complex analysis of good and evil in the contemporary world enables us to understand the underlying assumptions which shape moral judgement in the world of simulation. This chapter will examine Baudrillard's unconventional definitions of good and evil, exploring how he sees the dualistic conflict between them playing itself out in the contemporary world.

The relentless positivity of the global

Ours is a world, Baudrillard argues, that is already 'beyond good and evil'. This is not, however, in the sense that Nietzsche envisaged of the opening up of human potential through liberation from the constraints of Christian morality.[3] Rather, it is more the case that the poles of morality have collapsed into an insipid definition of 'the Good'. 'We can no longer speak Evil',[4] he notes. In hyperreality we are constrained by a relentless positivity, an overwhelming dominance of the Good. This is driven by the unquestioned sense of the good of the Western liberal capitalist system and our inability to question the innate goodness of growth and increased consumer realization. Thus Baudrillard defines the Good (as we perceive it in the contemporary world) as an excess of gratification, 'the belief that everything is granted us virtually, or will be, by the grace of continual growth and acceleration – including by extension, a universal lifting of prohibitions, the availability of all information and, of course, the obligation to experience *jouissance*'.[5] This is the religion of the consumer age; it is our redemption narrative. The death of God, he argues delivered us from responsibility to 'another world', but it has left us with a self-imposed responsibility to *this* world that overwhelms us. Redemption has changed its meaning: 'it is no longer the redemption of man and his sin, but the redemption of the death of God. That death has to be redeemed by a compulsive effort to transform the world'.[6] Baudrillard sees this as the next stage in the fusing of the capitalist and religious projects. Max Weber described the process of transforming of the world into wealth for the glory of God.[7] But now it is no longer a question of God's glory, 'it is a question of his death and of exorcizing it. The point is to make the world transparent and operational by extirpating from it any illusion and any evil force'.[8] Thus the contemporary quest for the Good is not so much constructive as crazed. Here Baudrillard's argument develops out of the pronouncement of the death of God by Nietzsche's 'madman' who bombards us with frantic questions about humanity's response to the murder it has committed: 'How can we console ourselves, the murderers of all murderers . . . who will wipe this blood from us? With what water could we clean ourselves . . . Is the magnitude of this deed not too great for us? Do we not ourselves have to become gods merely to appear worthy of it?'[9] Baudrillard conceives much human activity and our desire to shape the world as the strivings of this madman. The powerful forces of global transformation – markets, military interventions, democratic elections, consumerism – are all conceived in this Nietzschean sense as an irrational atoning compulsion to justify ourselves in a world after God.

Thus it is clear that, in Baudrillard's lexicon, 'the Good' is used, not so much as a moral category, but as a label for the popular understanding of *what makes life good* and comfortable. Obviously, Baudrillard views this as very far from good. Our fixation with 'the Good' is what is leading to the disappearance of humanity as we know it. 'Profusion is a kind of fatality – especially when people are overwhelmed, like the sorcerer's apprentice. They are not overcome by the malicious forces that they have unleashed, but by the best things they have created, the forces of Good that they have unleashed'.[10] And so, paradoxically, in the hyperreal world of the safe, the hygienic, the world of prodigious consumption, 'Now you must fight against everything that wants to help you'.[11]

Given this understanding of the Good, Baudrillard also uses the term 'Evil' in an atypical way. As we use it in popular discourse, he describes Evil as 'just a mask that we contrast with the Good that we are supposed to defend'.[12] Thus he notes the popular association of evil with terrorism, the most frequently identified threat to our way of life. In his own writing he also uses the term as defining this ideological 'other'. But he sees Evil as more integral to the system of the Good. At times, his usage does seem to carry the traditional moral sense, as when he seeks to unmask our understanding the Good as malicious: 'This absolute Evil comes from an excess of Good, an unchecked proliferation of Good, of technological development, of infinite progress, of totalitarian morality, of a radical will to do good without opposition. This Good turns into its opposite, absolute Evil'.[13]

More often, however, Evil is viewed, not as a morally insidious force, so much as a morally ambivalent deconstructive force present within the system, even as a source of social critique. Thus, in *The Transparency of Evil*, Evil is described as an underlying source of disruption, present throughout the simulations of contemporary culture:

> Beneath the transparency of the consensus lies the opacity of Evil – the tenacity, obsessiveness and irreducibility of the evil whose

contrary energy is at work everywhere: in the malfunctioning of things, in viral attacks, in the acceleration of processes and in their wildly chaotic effects, in the overriding of causes, in excess and paradox, in radical foreignness, in strange attractors, in linkless chains of events.[14]

An often cited example of this kind of 'evil' which undermines the smooth functioning of the Good is that of the 'virus', both the virtual viruses that sabotage computer systems and the biological viruses that have been the frequent topic of false pandemic scares over the last few years.[15] Under this umbrella of 'Evil', Baudrillard links the notion of the virus closely to the idea of terrorism as another viral force whose power is exerted as much through fear as through real danger. 'We know that terrorism will not overthrow the world order. Its impact is much more subtle: a viral and elusive form that it shares with world power'.[16] And so we have these combined Evil forces of terrorism and the virus: 'The virus of terror and the terror of viruses'.[17]

Similarly Baudrillard describes 'radical foreignness' as a manifestation of Evil in our homogenized world. An example of this might be the extreme antipathy felt towards immigrants in Western nations, who are felt not to conform in certain ways. We might also identify the enduring prejudice of racism which continues to shape public discourse. But, at the global level, Baudrillard sees this principle of Evil as embodied in states that reject the Western development model, both economically and also in terms of the liberalization of culture. Writing in the 1980s, Baudrillard describes how, through the Iranian Revolution and the Salman Rushdie affair, Ayatollah Khomeini came to be a powerful symbol of this phenomenon. He represents 'the negation of all Western values – of progress, rationality, political ethics, democracy and so on. By rejecting the universal consensus on all these Good Things, Khomeini became the recipient of the energy of Evil, the Satanic energy of the rejected, the glamour of the accursed share'.[18]

Other forms of Evil are less objectifiable. As we seek to make the world more predictable and rational, it is the forces of irrationality and instability that come under the label of Evil, even if these elements are integral to the system. Baudrillard alludes to a certain kind of vertiginousness or uncontrolled escalation that leads to chaos. Baudrillard died before the banking collapse of 2008, but many commentators have pointed to precisely this kind of excessive recklessness in the escalation of financial transactions that led to the collapse of the banking system. It seems that there is always the potential for us to lose confidence in the radical simulations of the hyperreal (in this case the simulations of capital) in such a way as brings the system crashing down.

These forms of Evil vary greatly. Some of them, such as violent terrorism, may be viewed as evil in the conventional sense. But these traditional moral categories are not of concern to Baudrillard here: 'The principle of Evil is not a moral principle but rather a principle of instability and vertigo, a principle of complexity and foreignness, a principle of seduction, a principle of incompatibility, antagonism and irreducibility. It is not a death principle – far from it. It is a vital principle of disjunction'.[19] As such a principle, Baudrillard insists that Evil cannot be viewed as a systematic opposition to Good. Only Good is, by definition, a system which is imposed on others. Evil is more of 'a deviance, a perversion. You never know where Evil is going or how'.[20] Drawing on President George W. Bush's designation of Iran, Iraq and Syria as an 'Axis of Evil' in his 2002 State of the Union Address (itself an evolution of Reagan's designation of the USSR as 'the Evil Empire')[21], Baudrillard argues that, 'Good is directive, directional; it has a finality in principle and therefore constitutes an axis . . . I do not see Evil as an identifiable axis embodied by men or organizations to be fought, but as an irrepressible drive for revenge on the excesses of the Good'.[22] Despite the continual temptation to present opponents of the West (particularly terrorist organizations) as single, organized entities, Baudrillard's view of a diverse and fragmented opposition to the dominant system of global governance seems much more realistic.[23]

So what use or relevance has any of this to the theologian? Clearly Baudrillard uses the terminology of morality ('Good' and 'Evil') in an unconventional sense as tools to deconstruct the socio-political myths of hyperreality. But in so doing he is also passing subtler moral judgements on the way in which these signifiers of 'Good' and 'Evil' are used in the contemporary world. He plays on the fact that these very words have become simulacra whose referents have perversely shifted. We might see this as reminiscent of the Prophet Isaiah's similar condemnation: 'Woe to you who call evil good, and good evil; Who substitute darkness for light and light for darkness;

Who substitute bitter for sweet and sweet for bitter!'.[24] Like Isaiah, Baudrillard is particularly concerned to unmask the totalitarian way in which the powerful can operate through giving definition to the language of morality. 'Power exists solely by virtue of its symbolic ability to designate the Other, the Enemy, what is at stake, what threatens us, what is Evil'.[25] Through the history of the Church, the power to anathematize and designate people and activities as evil has been a crucial element in the ability of the Church to control, and even abuse, as in the anathematizing of women's religious movements in the Middle Ages.[26]

Baudrillard's use of the term Evil also draws on the ambivalent connotations of evil within the Biblical tradition itself. He points out that the evil act for which Adam and Eve were driven from the Garden of Eden was in fact 'the principle of knowledge'.[27] In drawing justification for his more positive understanding of Evil, he comments (perhaps facetiously) 'if indeed we were chased from the Garden for the sin of knowledge, we may as well draw maximum benefit from it'.[28] Yet this notion of the benefits of the Fall is one that has recurred in the Christian Tradition. Thomas Aquinas described the Fall from the Garden of Eden as the 'felix culpa' (blessed fault), an act of disobedience which itself is caught up in the divine plan for the outworking of good. Consistent with Baudrillard's own prioritizing of the ceremonial, this motif has its origins several centuries earlier in the Exsultet, the liturgical proclamation sung at the Easter Vigil, where the Fall is described as the 'happy fault, O necessary sin of Adam, which gained for us so great a Redeemer!'

This is part of a wider questioning of simplistic designations of good and evil in Baudrillard's work. He alludes frequently to the heresy of Manichaeism, the dualistic worldview taught by Mani (AD 216–77). At the root of Mani's disagreement with the mainstream Church was his contention that evil was a primal force in continual and irresolvable conflict with goodness. Darkness and evil cannot therefore be vanquished by light and goodness in the way that orthodox Christianity believes has been accomplished by Christ. This ongoing dualistic struggle is present in Baudrillard's reading of the world and in some ways he criticizes modern religion for not being sufficiently Manichaean, for not expressing the 'impossible exchange' of the material world with the immaterial. Religion has become 'a process of reconciliation'[29] rather than an antagonistic challenge to the constructs of reality. Thus modern religion, along with modern politics, is naive in its proposals for the eradication of evil. Indeed Baudrillard's view of a totalized system (discussed in Chapter 3) leads him to believe that the negative aspects of the system under which we live are as indispensable as what we consider to be positive: 'We tell ourselves, of course, that it would be far preferable to use the money that goes on the fabulous commissions paid for funding arms deals, or even on arms production, to reduce world poverty. But that is to jump to a hasty conclusion'.[30] Baudrillard questions whether, within our system of economic growth, it is possible to separate out 'good' economic expenditure from 'bad' in this idealistic way. So he inclines towards the Manichaean worldview: 'We find ourselves . . . between good and evil, in an irresolvable antagonism'.[31] There is a fundamental 'inseparability of good and evil'.[32] He is certainly correct that in the expanding field of ethical investment the distinction between what is a 'good' investment and what is a bad one is very far from clear cut. For example, when biofuels became an attractive ethical option for investors concerned about the sustainability of fossil fuels, the result was a 75% increase in global food prices with a devastating effect on the world's poor.[33]

Nonetheless, against this position he argues that Manichaeism runs the risk of 'contradicting the whole of our humanism'[34] and thus implies that the ability to discern good from bad is a necessary human enterprise. It seems more often that his polemic is concerned with the opening up of a deeper moral question than this binarism permits. In the example given above, if our processes of international poverty eradication are simply directed at setting poorer countries further down the road of economic growth and exploitation of the natural world that the 'developed' world has experienced, then Baudrillard questions whether this should really be considered as 'good' rather than just a further contribution to the 'generalized concreting-over of the land'.[35] In this case, as in so many others, the definitions of Good and Evil are set by the highly constrained system in which we operate. So he concludes in relation to this moral issue that the answer to this question 'is of less importance than the realization that there is no fixed point from which we can determine what is totally good or totally evil'.[36]

Globalization and the good

This opens up some fundamental questions of what we should see as the drivers of human flourishing in the world today and what it means for a society to develop. For some time, thinking in this area has been dominated by a model of societal development based on the year on year growth of Gross Domestic Product through participation in the global market. Some theologians have embraced this explicitly such as Michael Novak in his book *The Spirit of Democratic Capitalism* which sees Free Market capitalism as bringing the freedoms necessary for Christian culture to take root. 'If democratic capitalism were to perish from the earth', he warns, 'humankind would decline into relative darkness and Jews and Christians would suffer under regimes far more hostile to their liberties and their capacities'.[37] Under Novak's view, the model of economic growth permits for the flourishing of wider social goods such as we associate with the Gospel.

Baudrillard warns us against this kind of optimism. In his earliest works he identified economic growth and productivity as performing 'the social function of *myth*',[38] a redemption narrative for our age. Governments promote growth and productivity, perpetuating the universally accepted mantras that growth is essential for development and social mobility. However, Baudrillard disputes this, arguing that growth in fact 'reproduces and restores social inequality, privileges and disequilibria'.[39] Arguing against the popular liberal economist of the time, John K. Galbraith, Baudrillard argues that the system of growth 'stabilizes, *whatever the absolute volume of wealth*, at a point which includes *systematic inequality*'.[40] The decades since Baudrillard's writing have continued to provide evidence of this. Models of economic development have continued to be driven by the objective of growth in GDP, but Martha Nussbaum has recently argued that this has led primarily to increased wealth among elites, feeding inequality and a polarization of wealth.[41] Nonetheless, growth continues because it functions for our society as *myth*. Here Baudrillard inherits Roland Barthes' definition of myth (itself a development of Marx's concept of ideology) as the process by which the reality of the world is transformed into an image of the world that we find more reassuring than the truth. 'And this image has a remarkable feature: it is upside down'.[42] We convince ourselves that a system that is perpetuating inequality is actually doing the opposite. Barthes shares Baudrillard's view that this process is inseparable from the move towards a 'politics of signs' and a 'spectacle society' since 'it organizes a world which is without contradictions because it is without depth, a world wide open and wallowing in the evident'.[43]

This early suspicion of the unquestioned benefits of economic growth as the sole means of development led Baudrillard to identify the absurdities of the way in which Gross National Product is calculated. Recent years have seen a more mainstream questioning of the helpfulness of GDP as the measure of society's wellbeing.[44] But as early as 1970, Baudrillard points out that rather than measuring the *goods* society produces, GNP measures *everything quantifiable* that society produces, which is altogether different. Consequently, domestic labour, research and culture are all excluded, and much is measured that actually exists to mitigate social ills (e.g. health care to counteract the illness caused by pollution). As a result 'we are everywhere reaching a point where the dynamic of growth and affluence is becoming circular and generating only wheel-spin and where, increasingly, the system is exhausting itself in its own reproduction'.[45] The psychological dimensions of living and working within such a system, which gives such little space to apparently 'non-productive' elements such as relationship and family life, are finally beginning to be given some airing in public debate.[46] However, the dominance of the myth of productivity and its accompanying work ethic would seem to allow little scope for change.

These themes are further developed in Baudrillard's later work, suggesting that the globalization of the free markets stands in opposition to the furthering of human dignity. In one of his last essays before his death, *The Violence of the Global* (2002), he warns against the conclusion that globalization (of technologies, markets, tourism, information) goes hand in hand with what we might consider to be a more positive universality of values (human rights, freedoms, culture and democracy). Here Baudrillard's understanding of the 'universal' is reminiscent of the universality Alain Badiou associates with Christianity, particularly as found in the writing of St Paul. Badiou argues how St Paul articulates a fundamental understanding of the human subject as bearer of universal truth, rooted in transcendent attributes and values. He suggests that this constitutes an unprecedented step towards subjectivity, 'subtracting truth from the communitarian grasp, be it that of a people, a city, an empire, a territory, or a social class'[47] and grounding it in the event of Christ's resurrection, the 'universal singularity'.[48] This universal subjectivity is grounded, therefore, not in subordination to any law, but in fidelity to the transcendent concepts of faith, hope and love.

In similar terms, Baudrillard looks back to a culture of the Universal, seemingly with some affection and nostalgia: 'a culture of transcendence, of the subject and the concept, of the Real and representation'.[49] However, he does not take the popular view (held by Novak) that globalization is an intrinsic propagator of this kind of universalism. He contends that the globalization of free market capitalism 'puts an end to the universality of values. It is the triumph of single-track thinking over universal thought . . . Democracy and human rights circulate just like any other global product – like oil or capital'.[50] In other words, free market capitalism will further the defence of human rights and democratic freedoms, only when it is economically expedient to do so. In many situations it has done the opposite, such as the way in which the opening up of the market for minerals in the Democratic Republic of the Congo to meet the Western demand for computer and mobile phone screens has fed the bloody civil war in that country.[51]

Baudrillard runs counter to conventional thinking here, where the expansion of free markets is believed to be the primary means of propagating democracy and respect for human rights around the world. On the contrary, to him these forms of universality seem more closely allied to the Evil that challenges the order of global power:

> Once the universal has been crushed by the power of the global and the logic of history obliterated by the dizzying whirl of change, there remains only a face-off between virtual omnipotence and those fiercely opposed to it. Hence the antagonism between global power and terrorism – the present confrontation between American hegemony and Islamist terrorism being merely the visible current twist in this duel between Integral Reality of power and integral rejection of that same power.[52]

There are undoubtedly questions to be raised about Baudrillard's globalization/universality dichotomy. Even Marxist Antonio Negri acknowledges that participation in the market has, in some sense, furthered the cause of equality for women and minority groups.[53] And while we may support his refusal to collude in the labeling of Islam in general as 'evil', the reality of life under Islamist regimes such as Iran and Saudi Arabia is appallingly repressive for many sections of society. Characteristically, Baudrillard over-eggs the pudding. But he does shed light on the ideological manner in which globalization is both championed and opposed.

Theological responses to globalization need to take this into account, discerning those universalizing forces that have brought about human flourishing and those which have fed violence and repression. Ecclesiology is one area where there is much discussion today of the relationship between the global and the local, but frequently little discussion about the character of the global power that has spread Christianity and with which it is, in various ways, associated. In Badiou's work we have seen how Christianity promoted a positive and empowering sense of the universal, of subjectivity and equality. But there is a darker side to this history too. As Christianity has spread, cultural practices and identities have been unnecessarily subordinated to a globalized interpretation of the Gospel, one based largely on the values of the West and, implicitly, on its economic system. Baudrillard alludes to the association of Christian missionary activity with economic globalization when he labels as 'heretical' anything that opposes 'the mission of the West . . . to subject the many different cultures, by any means available, to the unforgiving law of equivalence'.[54]

There is a continuing need to face up to this legacy and to disassociate Christianity from subjugating forms of global power, be that a particular economic system or an implicitly colonialist way of operating. William Cavanaugh suggests that the growth of the Church need not take the form of the imposition of any external system. He cites Henri de Lubac's contention that, for the Early Church Fathers, catholicity meant 'a gathering together rather than a spreading out, a cohesion around a centre that unites the disparate elements in their very diversity'.[55] This kind of mission sustains the positive Christian understanding of the universal. It gives dignity to human beings both through their connection to the transcendent and through their relationship with the diverse global Church. But, in its cultural openness, it resists the monocultural and oppressive forces of the global. Such is an authentic encounter with

Christ. Indeed, Cavanaugh goes on to argue that 'only Christianity satisfactorily solves the problem of the One and the many, because Christ is the "concrete universal". Only in the Incarnation can an individual be universal and the universal be individual'.[56]

If Baudrillard is right that in the age of global power, labour, human rights and democracy all circulate like capital in the generalized exchange, part of the theological challenge will be to defend the universals that flow from a belief that all human beings are created in God's image and that God became incarnate as a human individual. Furthermore that dignity will be grounded in a belief that human beings do not flourish through the individualism of competitive consumer capitalism but as interdependent people, expressed in a Church that does not impose its systems on diverse cultures. Here there needs to be a repentant recognition of the Church's contribution to the homogenization of global culture into what Baudrillard terms 'the Good'. There may even need to be a realization that much of what may be easily labelled as 'Evil' in the world today might in fact represent a more welcome challenge to a global power that debases human relationship and dignity.

8

Barred bodies

Americans may have no identity, but they do have wonderful teeth.[1]

Theological reflection on the body, gender difference and sexuality has seen dramatic growth in recent years. A diverse range of feminist and queer theologies have arisen, reflecting the increased preoccupation of the Church and other faith communities with issues of gender and sexuality in the contemporary world. The changing role of women and the increased acceptance of homosexuality have yet to be fully interpreted or accepted theologically. Both these dilemmas involve basic questions of the interpretation of Scripture and the development of tradition. But both are also significant in focussing immense questions of church order and holy living onto the locus of reality as we experience it: the human body. These conflicts within the Church can be so acrimonious and personally costly because external tensions about gender and sexuality are internalized within the bodies of individuals. Baudrillard sees the internalization of external systems within the human body as a defining attribute of our phase of advanced capitalism. This chapter will examine this central significance of the body in contemporary society as a site of division. I will then draw on his more ambivalent account of the body as site of symbolic negotiation to point to ways forward in the current theological debates.

Body as sacred consumer object

From his earliest work, Baudrillard identifies the body as playing a key role within the consumer system. As we have seen, for Baudrillard, society has become a 'system of objects' in which the sign value of the object has replaced any meaningful sense of use or exchange value. In explicitly religious language, Baudrillard identifies the body as the central object in this system, the object that has today achieved the status of 'an object of salvation. It has literally taken over that moral and ideological function from the soul'.[2] So the body is objectified and externalized from the 'true self' in its functional designation as capital (to be invested in and managed to the individuals' profit and gain). But most importantly it is fetishized as the supreme consumer object, the object which contains the greatest capacities for gratification and the sating of desire.

Formerly the assertion of the physicality of the body had been subversive, a challenge to the perceived anti-materialist priorities of religion. The Church became anxious to censor authors such as D. H. Lawrence who explored the passions of the flesh.[3] But in this new mythologized sense, Baudrillard argues, the body no longer constitutes its historic challenge to the metaphysical:

> The cult of the body no longer stands in contradiction to the cult of the soul: it is the successor to that cult and heir to its ideological function. As Norman O. Brown says in Life Against Death: 'We must not be misled by the antinomy of the sacred and the secular, and interpret as "secularisation" what is only a metamorphosis of the sacred'.[4]

In this contemporary 'sacralizing' of the body as both capital and consumer object, the drives of beauty and eroticism are central. In the consumption of the body, both by the self and by others within the marketplace, the ability to compete in these two areas of functionality is essential. Again Baudrillard employs religious language:

> For women, beauty has become an absolute, religious imperative. Being beautiful is no longer an effect of nature or a supplement

to moral qualities. It is the basic, imperative quality of those who take the same care of their faces and figures as they do of their souls. It is a sign, at the level of the body, that one is a member of the elect, just as success is such a sign in business.[5]

Beauty is here cast as a form of capital and the individual's commitment to enhancing the beauty of his or her body is described in the language of the Protestant work ethic as attainment of the signs of election and salvation. This quest for beauty runs in tandem with the imperatives of eroticism which 'orientates the "rediscovery" and *consumption* of the body today'.[6] The sexually attractive body is the competitive consumer object which has maximized its capital. But here Baudrillard is keen to draw the distinction between this functional erotic body that is the 'substrate of the exchanged signs of desire', meeting the social functions of eroticism, and the authentic body that is the 'site of fantasy and abode of desire'.[7] This distinction might be seen as that between the reality of the human body and the abstraction of the fashion model whose body 'is no longer an object of desire, but a functional object, a forum of signs in which fashion and eroticism are mingled . . . It is no longer, strictly speaking, a body, but a *shape*'.[8]

The drive to turn the body into an abstraction of beauty and eroticism that can compete within the sign economy is witnessed in the huge increase in cosmetic surgery. Given the urge behind such surgery to construct a 'hyperreal' body which expresses the self in the age of mass sign exchange, it is unsurprising (if disturbing) that cosmetic surgery has become a popular theme for so-called 'reality television'. Mirroring the explosion of 'extreme makeover' reality TV in the United States, British television has recently aired programmes such as *Cosmetic Surgery* on Channel Five, *Sun, Sea and Silicone* on Sky One and *10 Years Younger* on Channel Four. Baudrillard views reality television as a construction of reality, or rather as the construction of simulacrum, real in the order of digitalized hyperreality. There is something inevitable, therefore, in the way in which these programmes bring the construction of the hyperreal into the realm of the human body. They constitute the surrendering of the self to the manipulations of the sign economy in the pursuit of functional beauty and eroticism. In this sense, cosmetic surgery has little to do with the popular rhetoric around the actualization of a true self requiring expression. Mark Poster concludes:

> . . . participants in the shows alter themselves to mimic external standards either of celebrities or of the medical image of beauty. They change in unforeseen ways. They go down a road with no signposts and no predictable destination. They are not actualizing themselves, achieving their 'true' identity, but exploring possibilities of personhood in the age of information machines.[9]

The barred body

That the commodification of the body should have reached the point of surgical incision would also be of little surprise to Baudrillard, since he argued that the effect of the sign economy on the body was essentially one of barring and segmenting. The true beauty of the body is its symbolic value and its interactions with others through symbolic exchange. So just as in the general shift from symbol to sign where there is a reduction to digitality, so in the commodification of the body there is a reduction through segmentation, a metaphorical dismemberment. This has taken place through the modern era's long process of designating the body according to binary opposites (male/female, masculine/feminine, heterosexual/homosexual). But Baudrillard argues that in the sign economy, this process becomes inscribed on the body itself through the marking and dividing of the body into different anatomical parts:

> Ankle boots and thigh boots, a short coat under a long coat, over the elbow gloves and stocking-tops on the thigh, hair over the eyes or the stripper's G-string, but also bracelets, necklaces, rings, belts, jewels and chains – the scenario is the same everywhere: a mark that takes on the force of a sign and thereby even a perverse erotic function . . . under the structural form of a bar.[10]

This 'barring' deconstructs the body into zones (which Baudrillard would prefer to view as eroticized more than erogenous) replacing the body's symbolic significance with an accumulation of coded signs.

It is worth noting that much of contemporary medicine operates according to a similar segmenting effect, treating parts of the body in isolation and disregarding the interrelatedness of the whole. Baudrillard's description of the barring of the body through signs is often difficult to interpret, particularly in his use of the Freudian/ Lacanian symbolism of castration and phallic imagery. But what it amounts to is the belief that the way in which bodies are frequently presented in contemporary society reduces their full symbolic significance and takes the character of a kind of 'dismembering' through reduction to signs. There seem to be many representations of this in the popular media: a chain of London gyms recently ran a series of bill board advertisements encouraging the consumer to 'construct their perfect body' showing a muscular mannequin of a dismembered torso; many gyms offer classes focussing on specific body parts ('abs' or 'biceps'); cosmetic products designed to enhance specific parts of the body abound; and the proliferation of erotic images on the internet all add to the sense of human body parts being presented for consumption. Andy Warhol's portrait of the artist Jean-Michel Basquiat also depicts this kind of fragmented, barred body. Depicted in red, Basquiat's semi-naked body is pulled apart in an assembly of frames focussing on linked sections of his body. Even stripped of clothes, his body is presented as barred, dismembered.

Dying of a drug overdose at just 27, Basquiat seemed to personify much of the media-fuelled superficiality of life in 1980s New York that Warhol is famous for depicting. This destructive side of the supposed sexual revolution is also the focus of Baudrillard's writing about the body. He suggests that when the human body is caught up in the kind of consumer economy where all is available and nothing is denied, something fundamental is lost from the symbolic interactions of sex and the self that is formed through these rituals. In reading the implications of this kind of barring of the human body, Baudrillard takes up Lacan's language of the 'barred subject' in which the symbolic ambivalence of the body has been reduced to functionalities in which the genital function takes a primary role. In what Baudrillard describes as the 'Phallus Exchange Standard', the barred body is constrained within the male dominated social order with 'the Phallus becoming the absolute signifier around which all erogenous possibilities come to be measured, arranged, abstracted and become equivalent. The *Phallus exchange standard* governs contemporary sexuality in its entirety'.[11] Thus all sexuality becomes the simulation of the phallus. Each mark and sign on the body (whether male or female) is an imaginary or subconscious representation of the penis. All this means that Baudrillard sees little to celebrate in the supposed emancipation of sex and the liberation of female sexuality. Merely 'annexed to the phallic order', he writes, the barred female body is condemned to non-existence.[12] Germain Greer has recently made a similar argument in her discussion the 'manmade woman' in *The Whole Woman*, a work that constitutes a similar questioning of some of the supposed victories of the earlier feminist movement.[13]

So the barring of the human body has brought about a far less healthy sexual culture than popular opinion might hold. William Pawlett summarizes the dilemma:

> All sexuality is fetishistic because it focuses on partial objects: lips, eyes, bottoms, boots, stockings. We never confront the other in its fullness and radical otherness. The barred body of a man has hunky shoulders, toned arms and pecs, a grin. The barred body of a woman has breasts, long legs and long hair, a come-hither stare. But the situation is not equivalent because men fetishise woman to a far greater extent than women fetishise men.[14]

From sexual difference to transsexuality

This reductionist view gives the body a fundamental artificiality, a theme that Baudrillard takes up in relation to gender and the measures of sexual difference. Baudrillard's earlier work reflects the predominant view among theorists at the time that gender is fundamentally a construction and that removal of social influences on gender identity would bring about men and women who were essentially the same, certainly not restricted to particular roles and character types. In *For a Critique of the Political Economy of the Sign*, he writes:

> No being is assigned by nature to a sex. Sexual ambivalence (activity-passivity) is at the heart of each subject, sexual differentiation is registered as a difference in the body of each subject and not as an absolute term linked to a particular sexual organ.[15]

This position, with its feminist assumptions, was radically called into question, however, by Baudrillard's 1979 work, *Seduction*. His central thesis that the feminist revolution has marked the loss of something important in our society's processes of symbolic exchange – an element he labels 'seduction' – has resulted in the accusation that this book is 'an affront to feminism'[16]. In characteristically provocative style, Baudrillard seems to question the very premise of feminist liberation that the patriarchal society has subjugated women. 'The "traditional" woman's sexuality was neither repressed nor forbidden. Within her role she was entirely herself; she was in no way defeated, nor passive, nor did she dream of her future "liberation"'. He contends that the female has always exerted her own strategy, 'the unremitting, winning strategy of challenge' and that 'at each moment of the story the game was played with a full deck, with all the cards, including the trumps. And men did not win, not at all'.[17] There is, as ever, ambiguity in what Baudrillard is saying, but this should certainly not be read as a conservative reassertion of patriarchy on the grounds that women can be content with a kind of control of men exercised through their feminine wiles.

The first thing to note is that seduction, as Baudrillard uses the term here, is not simply a woman's exploitation of her own femininity in order to manipulate a man. As we saw in Chapter 3, it is a fundamental element in any kind of subversive strategy, including the political. Baudrillard explicitly states that he is not talking about 'the seduction to which women have been historically confined' but rather 'seduction as an ironic, alternative form, one that breaks the referentiality of sex and provides a space, not of desire, but of play and defiance'.[18] As such, we need to recognize that Baudrillard's use of the category 'feminine' here is in fact a continuation of his view that gender is a set of ambivalent qualities that should not be confined to biologically designated gender. He is speaking of 'feminine' as a more generalized quality.

But this understanding of seduction does indeed undermine much feminist theory if liberation for women is seen simply as the adoption of the stereotyped male identity. Baudrillard is not alone in suggesting that some feminists have themselves thought far too much in male terms, overlooking the aspects of femininity that are unique to women, such as childbirth, and the attributes that might spring from them.[19] So his critique here is directed primarily at the loss of a kind of dynamic tension in male/female relations that was conducive to the games and rituals of the symbolic order. He may have taken some inspiration here from Hegel's *The Phenomenology of Mind* where the parable of the Lord and the Bondsman serves to illustrate that the supposed underdog contributes much to the dynamic principle of historical progress. Baudrillard argues that the role of seduction is to annul power relations: does the man seduce the woman or does she seduce him? Seduction is more complex than a simple power relation and thus it is intrinsic to the symbolic. In the reductions of our sign economy these more subtle, ambivalent dimensions of human sociality are eradicated in what could be described as the total triumph of the masculine order, rather than the liberation of women: 'in this society, femininity is naught but the signs with which men rig it up'.[20]

It is also worth noting how much these kinds of questions have come to the fore in the time since Baudrillard wrote *Seduction*. Today there are contentious debates about how genuinely women have been liberated in the consumer society of the Western world, particularly as our culture interacts with the more conservative social structures of resurgent Islam. Is a woman who spends a fortune on cosmetic surgery and beauty treatments and conforms to the current definition of what is fashionable in women's dress really more empowered than the educated Muslim woman who chooses to wear the hijab? Is her life any less dictated to by social pressures and male-defined expectations?

So Baudrillard's understanding of gender is complex, embracing the essential suspicion of gender fixities that has characterized postmodern thought, but unafraid to use various polarities of gender in his quest for the symbolic. Indeed it is the collapse of these polarities into the play of signs that characterizes what he sees as the complete artificiality of gender identity today. In an article written in 1987 he provocatively declared 'We are all transsexuals now'.[21] By this he means that the fragmentation and semiotic reduction of the body have accelerated to the point where 'it is the body's destiny to become a prothesis'.[22] This artificiality is again driven by the way in which the body is caught up in the circulation of consumer objects and our bodies are driven to superficial competition:

What we look for today, where the body is concerned, is not so much health, which is a state of organic equilibrium, but fitness, which is an ephemeral, hygienic, promotional radiance of the body – much more a performance than an ideal state – which turns sickness into failure. In terms of fashion and appearance, we no longer pursue beauty or seductiveness, but the 'look'.[23]

Baudrillard sees the transsexual as embodying our current state of artificiality and gender indifference in two senses. First, of course, in the sense that we have lost any profound notion of what gender difference might mean and we have lapsed into the superficial, caricatured signs of gender that make up the barred body. These are particularly exaggerated in transsexuals who, Baudrillard suggests, 'live by the exaggerated, carnivorous signs of sexuality'.[24] But more controversially he argues that the indifference is to sex itself. Amidst the very saturation of sexualized marketing and pornographic images in our culture, we have become indifferent to sex in its true form, its *jouissance*, its potential to overwhelm our physicality. As a theologian might say, it has lost its sacredness. So it is in this context that we are left considering the vexed questions of gender identity to which science, sociology and psychology are still only providing us with partial answers: 'Once the orgy was over, sexual liberation could be seen to have had the effect of leaving everyone searching for their gender, their sexual and gender identity, with fewer and fewer possible answers, given the circulation of signs and the multiplicity of pleasures'.[25]

These insights do perhaps throw some light on the context in which the Church today is asking questions relating to gender difference and sexuality. They point to the anxiety generated by the loss of traditional boundaries, both in terms of sexual activity and gender roles. Baudrillard suggests that there are legitimate questions to be raised about whether the role of women within the Church should be inherently the same as that of men. He highlights the confusion present in a society that normalizes sexual activity outside of marriage. But Baudrillard is also considering these issues at a far deeper level than is commonly found in the Church. In particular he asks the crucial question of whether gender characteristics need to be mapped universally across biologically determined gender categories. Can there not be a wider array of types and, therefore, vocations within the genders that goes beyond a binary distinction? And if this is the case, how might all Christians (particularly those in a representational ministry of the Church) need to call into question assumptions and stereotypes about their own gender? For example, if we were to conceive of priesthood as encompassing both the receptive Christ-bearing of Mary and the active authority of Peter (though such stereotypes would themselves need to be challenged in relation to these figures), then priests of both genders would need to expand their self-understanding to exercise the full charisms of the priestly ministry.

In any event, it would surely be insightful to place the Church's questions about homosexuality and gender within the wider picture of the impoverishment of both sex and gender in the consumer culture. Perhaps the conservative entrenchment on these issues is as much (if not more) a reaction to the loss of something fundamental in both these areas of contemporary life than grounded in reasoned argument on these particular issues. Perhaps we would move beyond current impasses if our focus shifted to the greater task of the recovery of the sacredness and *jouissance* of sex *per se* and the essential ambivalence and nuance of gender difference.

Sacramental body

We can see that Baudrillard identifies great problems in contemporary society's approach to the body, gender and sex. But his agenda would wrongly be interpreted as a conventionally conservative one. His critique of sexuality in the sign economy is not a defence of bourgeois morality and he would have little in common with those who would want to resolve the Church's current confusions over gender and sexuality through a reassertion of conservative positions. For Baudrillard the body's essential ambivalence and fluidity must be preserved against both the constrictive binarisms of modernity (including gender difference as conventionally conceived) and its current semiotic reduction. He shares in the critiques of any notion of 'natural law' that would identify overarching, normative types of human identity and behaviour, generalities to which particular people should conform. However, he would claim that there is a naivety in thinking that, once the body is freed from the constrictions of received natural law, our contemporary culture permits a somehow unregulated expression of the body. On the contrary, Baudrillard is equally resistant to the pornographizing, phallicizing of the semiotic barring we witness in consumer culture. Baudrillard would remove the 'semiotic bar' that fixes identities according to any kind of culturally determined label, whether defined by the Church or the diktats of the fashion system. Rather, human identity should be received and re-conceived within the operations of symbolic exchange. This symbolic negotiation of identity is not a negotiation 'by the subject behind the mask, nor the manipulation of the sign: on the contrary it consumes the subject's identity and, like the subject, enters the game of possession and dispossession, the entire body becoming, just like the gods and women, material for symbolic exchange'.[26]

This emphasis on the significance of the body in its physicality and within its symbolic interactions resonates with how the body is reconceived, even symbolically regenerated, within the symbolic interactions of liturgy. Baptism enacts the consuming of the candidates' identities within the dispossession that is participation in the death of Christ. The body is then repossessed and renewed through participation in Christ's resurrected life. This is also a rebirth into the body of the community, the Church. Similarly the Eucharist is a symbolic renegotiation of identity through the body's participation in a corporate feeding that again participates in the dispossession and regeneration of Christ's passion. The body is reconceived through symbolic exchange with others. Questions of individual labelling (gender and sexuality) are relativized through the incorporation into a greater social body: 'though we are many, we are one body, because we all share in one bread'.

The key symbol at the centre of both these sacraments is the offering of Christ's own body, an action which many have argued does relativize various aspects of Jesus' own identity. Graham Ward argues that the iconicity of the crucified body 'does not erase the physical but overwhelms it, drenching it with significance. The maleness of Christ is made complex and ambivalent, in the way that all things are made ambivalent as their symbolic possibilities are opened up by their liminality'.[27] He observes how the medieval church felt it appropriate to identity femininity in Christ's body at this moment, particular as a mother, with the wounded side representing both the lactating breast and the womb from which the Church is born. Furthermore, through our sacramental participation in this intensely significant bodily offering, our bodies too 'will perform in ways which transgress the gendered boundaries of established codes'.[28] He makes particular reference to the relativizing of masculinity in the writings of Bernard of Clairvaux and Aelred of Rievaulx and of femininity in the writings of Mechtild of Magdeburg and Hadewijch.

Moving from gender to the expression of sexuality, Timothy Radcliffe has shown how this eucharistic image of the body given in love might be the model of the Christian understanding of a body reconceived in its sexual encounters: 'If the giving of a body is the sacrament at the heart of our prayer then it is not surprising that one of the most profound ways in which we express who we are is by giving our bodies to someone else . . . [Sex] is a profoundly eucharist act'.[29] The obstacles he identifies to this full significance of sex are similar to Baudrillard's analysis in recognizing a certain kind of objectification of the body and an accompanying transactional view of sex. On the eucharistic model, Radcliffe suggests that Christian sexual ethics should be about 'living relationships of gift rather than of property exchange'.[30]

As in the Eucharist, the offering of our bodies in love to another is a dispossession that can lead to the regeneration of who we are. Within this context all fixities of gender and status are relativized. William Pawlett's reading of Baudrillard on sex is reminiscent of this ambivalent mystical moment:

'Sex' occurs in the spaces of exchange between ritual bodies; it is not a property, essence or resource of those bodies beyond the practice of ritual exchange. The person enclosed in symbolic relations is in a state of 'radical ambivalence' in relation to themselves and to others. Both self and other to our 'selves' and self and other to others: we never coincide with ourselves or with others, Baudrillard insists, we exchange with them. We are both 'male' and 'female', child and adult, good and evil: in a state of ambivalence, we are literally 'strong' on both sides of the bar. Here there is no identity, no fixity, no value, as the bar enabling these 'things' is annulled.[31]

In this sense it seems that the sexual/sacramental moment is some kind of experience of St Paul's 'lifting of the bar' in his ambiguous phrase that in Christ, 'there is no longer Jew or Greek, there is no longer slave or free, there is no longer male and female'.[32] These parallels with Pauline language can be taken further through passages of Baudrillard's work that indicate his concept of 'seduction' has much in common with Paul's understanding of grace. Notably, Baudrillard contrasts seduction with 'Law', suggesting that 'seduction comes from no longer recognizing the authority of the law, or the reality principle, the economic, moral, political, historical, etc. principle to something arbitrary'.[33] Overcoming this law-bound definition of ourselves seems to move us closer to receiving the body as gift in both its vulnerability and power. This leads to a radically deeper conception of the self: 'the fact that there is a transmutation that makes us pass to the other side of the law is a way of showing that it is possible to live as the image of the Other, somewhere other than in the law, on the other side'.[34]

What Baudrillard means here by 'the Other' will be explored further in Chapter 10, but suffice to say that the body conceived in this way is a body less manipulated by the semiotic reductions of our culture and more alive to a radically deeper significance. It is perhaps a recovery of what Rowan Williams has called 'the body's grace'. In more Christian language, the 'transmutation through seduction' that Baudrillard identifies might be described as a fundamental understanding of the body in relation to God: 'a transformation that depends in large part on knowing yourself to be seen in a certain way: as significant, as wanted'.[35]

9

Fragments in the desert

Welcome to the Desert of the Real.[1]

Baudrillard's entire corpus can be seen as a great elaboration of Marshall McLuhan's famous dictum 'the medium is the message'.[2] It is not merely the content of his writing that should be considered (indeed over-analysis is often counterproductive!) but also his manner of writing. In this sense, his work is performative. His move away from structuralist theory towards a less formal writing style is his very message of the breakdown of the Real. Baudrillard is interested in the business of writing itself:

> Ideological and moralistic critique, obsessed with meaning and content, obsessed with the political finality of discourse, never takes into account writing, the act of writing, the poetic, ironic, allusive force of language, of the juggling with meaning. It does not see that the resolution of meaning is to be found there – in the form itself, the formal materiality of expression.[3]

This chapter will explore this 'formal materiality of expression' in Baudrillard's work and considers its relation to theology under the three themes of the desert, the fragment and the poetic.

The desert of the real

In the history of Christianity, much wisdom has come to us from the desert. The collected sayings of men and woman dedicated to religious life in the deserts of Egypt from the mid-third centuries constitutes the most significant body of pre-modern Christian wisdom after the New Testament. The influence of the desert tradition on St Benedict brought the wisdom of the desert fathers and mothers into the fabric of the Western spiritual life. These writings are very different from the scholastic Christian philosophy that would follow it in the Middle Ages. Here we do not find the systematic interrogation of Christian truth that would be exemplified in Thomas Aquinas' *Summa Theologica,* nor the totalized outworking of Christian practice in the Gregorian enterprise of Canon Law. The wisdom of the desert has less all-encompassing and universal aspirations. In its aphorisms, images, fables and verse it seeks only to shine lights on a truth before which it stands in humility. Like the desert itself, truth is a space which can never be fully tamed, navigated and exploited. It is simply to be cautiously and respectfully inhabited.

In our contemporary world, the desert is growing. In 2007, the United Nations declared desertification 'the greatest environmental challenge of our times'.[4] A combination of climate change and the overexploitation of land is leading to the increasing aridity of much previously fertile land, particularly in sub-Saharan Africa and central Asia. So, as a key contemporary trend, it is unsurprising that the desert should also be a theme in Baudrillard's writing, not least that written during his years in the deserts of California. For Baudrillard, the desert is of a metaphorical significance that extends beyond the desert places themselves into the culture of a whole society. In hyperreality, he argues, 'the towns and villages are not a refuge from the desert, they give the desert sanctuary'.[5] This metaphor of the desert is used in Baudrillard's writing in two contrasting senses.

First there is the negative connotation of the desert as an arid place where there is little life and growth. This is Baudrillard's famous 'desert of the real' which symbolizes the vacuous superficiality of the hyperreality he describes in his work. The desert is a metaphor for late consumer capitalism, stripped of symbolic exchange, of meaningful interaction and social dynamism. 'The desert is a sublime form that banishes all sociality, all sentimentality, all sexuality'.[6] The growth of the desert therefore symbolizes a kind of cultural desertification which he saw exemplified in the United States where, he argues, 'you cannot differentiate between a desert and a metropolis'.[7] 'For us the whole of America is a desert. Culture exists there in a wild state: it sacrifices all intellect, all aesthetics in a process of literal transcription to the real'.[8] As well as a kind of cultural aridity, the desert also represents Baudrillard's characteristic themes of the reductions of time and space. The desert is a place of spatial and temporal distortion, primarily because it lacks any centre or point of orientation; it is merely criss-crossed by freeways where high-speed motor travel distorts the relationship between space and time. So the infinitely extendible cities are fused with the deserts as a symbol of the fusing of culture and nature.

So Baudrillard's first conception of the desert is as the site of something lost. It seems to allude to the lost Eden (Genesis 3.23), the arid ground to which Adam and Eve were banished, ever to seek restoration. As such it is a place we might want to flee from in a contemporary account of redemption, or at least metaphorically journey through, just as the Israelites journeyed through the literal desert to seek the Promised Land. Conversion, for Michel de Certeau, is the 'crossing of a desert of meaning'.[9]

On the other hand, Baudrillard also appears to hold out some positive sense of the desert, reminiscent of Christian tradition of the desert as place of insight. This is the desert of Mount Sinai where desolation makes possible revelation. This biblical ambivalence towards the desert is also seen more broadly in Baudrillard's thought. He is characteristically ambivalent to hyperreality as both the loss of meaning but also the liberation from modernity's oppressive structures, and so he describes the desert as a source of fascination, precisely because it is a place where we are 'delivered from all depth'. In the severity of the desert landscape we experience 'a challenge to meaning and profundity, a challenge to nature and culture, an outer hyperspace, with no origin, no reference points.[10] Thus Baudrillard sees the desert as an implosion of the categories of natural and cultural which he perceives more widely in hyperreality. In an experience of the quasi-natural of the desert we are permitted some deeper connection with the experience of the quasi-cultural of the hyperreal.[11] It is a form of transcendence with a metaphysical quality:[

> The wonder of the heat is metaphysical. The very colours – pastel blue, mauve, lilac – are the products of a slow, geological, timeless combustion. The mineral quality of the earth breaks through the surface in the crystalline flora. All the natural elements here have known their ordeal by fire. The desert is no longer a landscape, it is a pure form produced by the abstraction of all others.[12]

In this transcending of nature and culture, Baudrillard finds in the desert a starkness and intensity of the hyperreal that seems to instil some new kind of critical attentiveness. This takes on particularly mystical language when he describes the desert as 'an extension of the inner silence of the body':

> If humanity's language, technology, and buildings are an extension of its constructive faculties, the desert alone is an extension of its capacity for absence, the ideal schema of humanity's disappearance . . . When you emerge from the desert, your eyes go on trying to create emptiness all around; in every inhabited area, every landscape they see desert beneath, like a watermark. It takes a long time to get back to a normal vision of things and you never succeed completely. Take this substance from my sight! . . . But the desert is more than merely a space from which all substance has been removed. Just as silence is not what remains when all noise has been suppressed. There is no need to close your eyes to hear it. For it is also the silence of time.[13]

The desert then also indicates some kind of clarity of vision. In a world saturated by the presence and circulation of objects, the desert represents radical absence, which is itself a presence underlying much of everyday experience. In this sense it is perhaps a spatial embodiment of the radical otherness (or Nothing) we shall come to consider in the next chapter. This theme naturally resonates with the apophatic tradition of mystical theology: that the divine might be encountered in a profound embracing of absence, a 'negativity of experience'[14] that embraces our absolute unknowing of God. Here Baudrillard associates the absence intrinsic to the desert ('take this substance from my sight!') with the deep silence of time.

Thus Baudrillard's conception of the desert also points towards the kind of mystical possibilities associated with the desert in the Christian tradition as a place of connection and meaning through the embracing of absence. Drawing on Michel de Certeau, David Jasper describes the journey into the desert as:

. . . a self-imposed exile from the solidity of things, yet into a harsh landscape that demands not less than everything. It demands a detachment and a silence that realises and is realised by a purely oxymoronic language, a language that feeds on otherness which, in its abysses and pitiless horizons, becomes a theatre of memory painfully assembling the fragments of lost unity that is the speech of God.[15]

Fragments

The most significant shift in Baudrillard's writing is from his earlier theoretic treaties which constitute recognizable contributions to the field of sociology (e.g. *Consumer Society* and *Symbolic Exchange and Death*), to the aphoristic fragments that make up his later works.[16] These are epitomized in the *Cool Memories* series which are collections of thoughts, reflections and diary entries from the late 1980s and 1990s. This shift in writing style may be understood, to some degree, as the radical embracing of a wider trend in contemporary thought. Postmodern thinkers have exposed the inadequacy (even potential totalitarianism) of 'grand narratives'. As Baudrillard writes, 'The deconstructive work has been done, you have to come to terms with it'.[17] Comparable to the cultural bricolage he describes, Baudrillard believes we live in an age where thought can only draw parasitically on its former great systems without embracing any of them in their totality. This is the postmodern shift from the universal to the particular. Baudrillard therefore turns his back on this grand systematizing in favour of an attentiveness to detail and particularity, seeking glimpses of truth where 'each moment, each phase is perfect in its incomparable singularity, the fruit is perfect, but no more perfect than the flower . . . [T]aken at the level of meaning, the world is pretty disappointing, but each detail of the world, taken in its singularity, is perfect'.[18] It is these small singularities of truth and clarity that Baudrillard seeks among the confusions and distortions of contemporary thought. In a sense, they deliver because they promise so little: '[These fragments] alone will survive the catastrophe, the destruction of meaning and language, like the flies in the plane crash which are the only survivors because they are ultra-light'.[19]

David Shield's book *Reality Hunger* adopts a similar style of intellectual and cultural bricolage. He assembles a series of unattributed citations along with his own thoughts and aphorisms in what he describes as a manifesto, 'the *ars poetica* for a burgeoning group of interrelated (but unconnected) artists in a multitude of forms and media (lyric essay, prose poem, collage novel, visual art, film . . .) who are breaking larger and larger chunks of reality into their work'.[20] This reality is not easily homogenized or synthesized. It cannot be seamlessly narrated: 'Modernism ran its course, emptying out narrative'.[21] So Shields endeavours merely to assemble thoughts and ideas, guiding us through themes and engaging his reader in their interpretation.

Both Shields and Baudrillard (in his later writing) narrate an unsystematic world in an unsystematic way. But unlike Shields', Baudrillard's voice is nearly always his own (with occasional citations from the likes of Lichtenberg and Nietzsche). While Shields presents the multiplicity of voices in our subjective free market of thought, Baudrillard more particularly reflects the dilemma of the contemporary philosopher or social commentator that no one can any longer assume 'the God's eye view'. There is no longer a dispassionate rational observer able to tell us 'how things are'. We are offered diary entries, notes and observations, insights into the philosopher's own life and psychology, all caught up in the complex systems and matrices of the hyperreal. They point to the sense that we are all constrained in our ability to make assessments of the Real and implicated in our criticisms. As such, criticism can only be less coordinated and systematically executed: ' . . . all radical criticism now belongs exclusively to the haphazard, the viral, the catastrophic – to accidental or system-led reversal'.[22] Thus in the fragmentary approach Baudrillard as writer self-consciously surrenders control over the interpretation of his writing to a multiplicity of readers. He describes fragmentary writing as 'ultimately democratic writing'. In their undeveloped and unsynthesized presentation, 'Each fragment enjoys an equal distinction. The most banal one finds its exceptional reader. Each, in its turn, has its hour of glory'.[23]

In this fragmented exploration of reality many boundaries are blurred, not least between what is objectively factual and what is creative or imagination-based. In Shield's approach, 'the subjectivity of the personal essay and the objectivity of the public essay . . . [are conflated] into a literary form that relies on both art and fact, on imagination and observation, rumination and argument, human faith and human perception'.[24] In both Shields and Baudrillard, the aphorism is a favoured genre, sometimes alluding to observation, analysis or theory, but frequently standing alone, provoking further thought in its very ubiquity. In Baudrillard's work this seems particularly inspired by Nietzsche's later writing, blurring myth and reality, sanity and insanity. But they are not nihilistic ramblings. There is intention and meaning behind them. Of this writing style Baudrillard writes, '"*Aphorizein*" (from which we get the word "aphorism") means to retreat to such a distance that a horizon of thought is formed which never again closes on itself'.[25]

The closing of horizons was the failing of modern thought systems, leading to absolutism and totalitarianism. In contrast, the aphorism maintains a certain humility before truth. It is a retreat in order to see the picture more fully without endeavouring to recapture it. It is perhaps for comparable reasons that aphorism is the predominant genre found in the Wisdom literature of the Hebrew Scriptures. Of all truths, God is that which is most resistant to reduction and objectification, and divine wisdom in human texts can only ever be pointers or ciphers towards truth. Aphorisms throw light onto the divine nature while never aspiring to illuminate the whole. It was this approach that was taken up by the Desert Fathers and Mothers and perhaps this is, therefore, a mode of theological writing ripe for revival, one which would better resonate with our culture than lengthy systematic tracts. Laurence Freeman writes how this kind of aphoristic desert wisdom might speak again to our age:

> The desert wisdom teaches rather than preaches. Its authority is experiential, not theoretical. The upshot of this is a phenomenon that many modern people, disenchanted with religious institutionalism, will find unusual – a religious group that is grasped by the absolute experience of God and is uncompromising in its desire to be one with that experience while remaining humorous,

humble and, above all, not condemning of those of other beliefs or practice.[26]

So it is the fragment (of which the aphorism is a favoured form) that represents Baudrillard's predominant later philosophical mode. Only the fragment constitutes the form of understanding proper to the desert of the Real, a world where signs and language have come adrift from their signifiers. But the fragment also carries something of the positive quality of the desert as a place of profound attentiveness and insight. His description of the fragment as singularity even carries a kind of sacramental quality as a sign (or symbol?) that points beyond itself and beyond the limits of understanding:

> The fragment is like a broken mirror – ideas don't have the time to reflect themselves in it or, as a result, to feel sorry for themselves. They run ahead of their shadows or their reflections.
>
> To run ahead is to move towards an unforeseeable outcome, but one whose path is made for it in advance. Birds too run ahead of those who see them. The event also runs ahead of history. It opens up untimely perspectives in a world brought totally up to date.[27]

In the fragment the idea is always ahead of its representation or reduction. Thus it is the fragment that has the potential to move us forward in discerning something of the truth within the hyperreal. Theologian David Tracy adopts a similar stance. Also drawing on Nietzsche, as well as Christian exponents of fragmentary wisdom such as Kierkegaard, Pascal, Walter Benjamin and Simone Weil, Tracy argues that fragments are the only response to our 'new global sense of polycentrism'.[28] For Tracy, postmodernity is the breaking of totality through 'explosions of once-forgotten, marginalized and repressed realities in Enlightenment modernity'.[29] Thus Tracy's use of the fragment is essentially a means of attending to the 'other', marginalized by the systems of modern thought. He views the fragment as reconstituting the potential for justice beyond the unavoidably exclusive definitions of modern political systems. Consequently, he, like Baudrillard, is not nostalgic for any lost totality nor nihilistic in his view of fragments. 'Fragments are our spiritual situation. And that is not so bad a place to be'.[30] Tracy shares Baudrillard's quasi-sacramental view of the potential of fragments and sees them in a similar way as the means of drawing us beyond the impasses of modern reductionism and the self-referentiality of the hyperreal:

> Let go of the hope for any totality system whatsoever. Focus instead on the explosive, marginalized, saturated and, at times, auratic fragments of our heritages . . . Blast the marginalized fragments of the past alive with the memory of suffering and hope; remove them from their seemingly coherent place in the grand narratives we have imposed on them. Learn to live joyfully, not despairingly, with and in the great fragments we do indeed possess.[31]

In criticism, one might argue that this kind of bricolage has a kind of 'in-built' nostalgia, that any fragment presupposes a system of thought that we implicitly mourn. In response to Tracy, Derrida has argued that the figure of the fragment implies a broken whole and in employing the fragment a thinker is occupying a position of authority since he is inevitably drawing on that system.[32] Here it must be said that Baudrillard's later fragmentary writing is particularly susceptible to the charge that his aphorisms allude constantly to, even recycle, his previous, more systematic work. Indeed it could be argued that his collections of aphorisms are something of a commentary on theory he has previously set out. Fragments may refer, for example, to his earlier writing on the reality of the Gulf War or the precession of simulacra and no meaning will be obvious to those unfamiliar with Baudrillard's core themes. However, it would be fairer to say that most fragments serve as illustrations of that earlier theoretical work and do, in that sense, stand alone. Rather than set out a framework through which people might look at the world to seek understanding, he presents those signs and experiences themselves as windows onto his themes of interpretation.

This is how Baudrillard might be seen more generally, not as the non-realist he is sometimes portrayed, but as a new kind of realist describing a 'less real' world. He does not present idealist theories through which we might interpret experience. He presents us with fragments of the Real to be taken for what they are and, as Tracy suggests, to point us to previously unseen or excluded perspectives on the way things are.[33] It is perhaps possible therefore to view the fragment, not so much as a broken whole for which we feel nostalgia, but as something perpetually (and quite properly) incomplete. In that sense the fragment may reflect an eschatological provisionality of thought which good theology always holds in mind. Whereas the systemic rationality of modernity constantly presented us with premature teleology, the final word on all things, the fragment points to the eschatological incompleteness that might be seen as the most valuable insight of postmodern thought.

Poetic resolution

Some of the fragments to feature in Baudrillard's later work (and even earlier theoretical work) were in fact fragments of poems he had written in his twenties and although he never returned to writing formal poetry, much of the fragmentary work has a strongly poetic quality. He had written a sequence of 17 poems in the 1950s[34] and a fragment of the tenth poem appears, for example, in *Seduction* as part of Baudrillard's discussion of the Renaissance decorative technique *trompe l'oeil*:

A clock without hands
imposes time but
leaves the hour to be divined.
Darkness is simple or
the contradictory one
of green curtains.
Water is soft to the touch
like a natural death.[35]

The poem conveys the liminality and superficiality of *trompe l'oeil* images (an early form of simulation) whose objects 'are approaching the black hole from which, for us, reality, the real world, and normal time emerge'.[36] But at the same time there is the tactile sensuality of water and the symbolic power of death. It is in *Symbolic Exchange and Death* that Baudrillard sets out his theoretical understanding of what he believes can be accomplished through poetry. In essence, the poetic does to language what symbolic exchange does to market exchange, that is to say it annuls value, law and productivity. Poems do not need to obey the conventional rules governing language (Baudrillard takes issue with Saussure on this point). Poetic language does not signify something better than prose could; it is 'irreducible to the mode of signification, which is nothing other than the mode of production of the values of language'.[37] Thus in its subversion of linguistic signification, poetry enables us to overcome the rational, productivist worldview based on value. It is 'the restitution of symbolic exchange in the very heart of words'.[38]

Poetry is therefore outside of the reductionism of the Code. It does not disclose everything but remains enigmatic and ambivalent. 'In the poetic text, it is infinite, because no code whatsoever can be found there, no deciphering is possible, and because there is never a signified to put an end to the cycle'. This implies that the language of a poem points to something more profound than the instrumental use of language, and it is here that the subversive capacity of poetry lies. For Baudrillard, a poem's ultimate signification is a negation: 'if the poem refers to something, it is always to NOTHING, to the term of nothingness, to the signified zero. Poetic intensity consists in the vertigo of this perfect resolution, which leaves the place of the signified or the referent perfectly empty'.[39] The theological implications of this kind of negativity will be explored in the next chapter. But it is worth noting here, in terms of language, how Baudrillard expresses all this in the language of *theocide*. The poetic puts to death of the name of God, but in such a way that the name continues to 'haunt the poem':

> [The poetic] is, *on the level of the signifier, of the name it incarnates, the equivalent of putting God or a hero to death in a sacrifice* . . . The name of God, torn limb from limb, dispersed into its phonemic elements as the signifier, is put to death, haunts the poem and rearticulates it in the rhythm of its fragments, without ever being reconstituted in it as such.[40]

From a Judeo-Christian theological perspective, two things are interesting about this theocidal definition of the poetic. First is the specification that poetry puts to death the *name* of God (a theme Baudrillard develops extensively in the final chapter of *Symbolic Exchange*). In the Book of Exodus, Yahweh ('I am who I am') is the God who refuses to be named and will be designated only in reference to his own being. God is not an idol precisely because

God will not be named. So the destruction of the name of God is an act of iconoclasm, an unmasking of idolatry to make space for the 'unnamed God'.[41] Jean-Luc Marion explores this in his quest for an understanding of God which expresses the iconicity of love rather than the conceptual idolatry of metaphysical being, and so Marion crosses out the word 'God' to dissociate the God of revelation from the God of metaphysics and morality.[42] Second, the brutality of this 'sacrifice' brings to mind Christological themes, particularly in the Girardian[43] sense that what is put to death on the cross is a distorted (and therefore idolatrous) understanding of a God who demands sacrifice. Again, to quote Marion, 'We are speaking of the God who is crossed by a cross because he reveals himself by his placement on a cross'.[44]

All of this implies, therefore, a connection between poetry and revelation, an area of some interest in contemporary theology. Much of this work points to the idea that, when it comes to speaking about God, less is often more, and ambiguity is less idolatrous than scientific clarity. Paul Fiddes, for example, suggests that 'a poem, containing a multiplicity of images, is characterized by compression of meaning. It hides meaning in order to find it again with increase'.[45] He cites Iris Murdoch: 'Philosophy is clarification, but art is mystification' in a way that is very evocative of Baudrillard's own shift from prose to poetic fragment. He too believes that his task is 'not to decipher, but to cipher'.[46] We might say that for Baudrillard the opposite of poetry is pornography where everything is displayed and nothing is seductive. This is the 'obscenity' of a culture saturated with information and explanation. In contrast, 'the poet deliberately "hides" his meaning through the use of image, but at the same time he knows he cannot control the expansion of meaning that takes place when he does so'.[47] Fiddes sees this approach in the Biblical Wisdom literature, a delight in what is incomprehensible and mysterious. He quotes from the Book of Proverbs:

Three things are too wonderful for me;
Four I do not understand:
The way of an eagle in the sky,
the way of a serpent on the rock,
the way of a ship on the high seas,
And the way of a man with a maiden.[48]

Extending the sexual metaphor and the characterization of contemporary culture as pornographic, Baudrillard describes our present time as living 'after the orgy'[49] of modernity. We might say that twentieth-century theology saw its own 'orgy' of exhaustive unmasking and systematizing. We have seen the long deconstructive process of historical criticism and the vast constructive systems of Barth, Rahner and Von Balthasar. On the one hand the scientific dissection of faith has left many wondering whether anything remains and on the other such great doctrinal systems have been constructed that they might themselves be described as self-referential hyperrealities, internally coherent but somehow cut adrift from the Real they seek to describe. It is no wonder that Paul Ricoeur (himself drawing parallels between the poetic and the revelatory) calls us to a 'second naiveté'.[50] In its use of poetry, the theological imagination 'thus reaches out towards mystery, towards a reality that is our final concern but which eludes empirical investigation and bursts rational concepts'.[51] This should not be an excuse for sloppy thinking in theology but merely a caution against the idolatries of concept and system and against the dangers of 'totalizing' the name of God. Baudrillard's work is a reminder that ours is not the only discipline where these dangers are present.

Although poetic fragments feature more strongly in Baudrillard's later work, it seems sad that he never returns to a more serious commitment to writing poems, favouring instead the artistic (and even more fragmentary) form of photography.[52] Perhaps even a whole poem is too totalized a narrative. In comparing his work to that of Julia Kristeva (whose work on the poetic and symbolic undoubtedly influenced Baudrillard), Mike Gane laments that Baudrillard is never fully able to embrace the symbolic: 'It is possible to see via Kristeva, that Baudrillard's language is a divided one: he cannot dispense with a semiotic register, and, although he seeks transfinite order in the poetic range, his purely poetic writings are never sufficient for his purposes'.[53] In a sense, the symbolic never really 'takes off' in Baudrillard's work. His fragments are perhaps too fragmented, too wedded to observational insights of what Gane calls the 'semiotic register'. For the theologian, fragments (poetic or otherwise) must point to something that will one day be whole, what Fiddes calls the theologian's 'final concern'. I believe we do live in the age of the fragment, the desert of the real. But that it not all there is.

10

Radical otherness

It is always better to depend in life on something that does not depend on us.[1]

The curious and distinctive feature of theology in comparison with other disciplines is that while it might be said to have an object of study (God), many of those who take theology most seriously believe that this is not a passive object but one that exerts its own agency on its subject. What is often at stake in academic theology today is the difference between a discipline of 'religious studies' which considers belief systems and faith communities historically, sociologically, anthropologically, etc., and a more ambitious theology which believes that truth is to be found in dynamic relation to the source of all observable matter. Thus, theology has always presented a challenge to the underlying premise of post-Enlightenment thought: the sovereign subject's authority over the observable object. This final chapter will explore how Baudrillard's work might illuminate our understanding of the subject/object relation in theology and other disciplines. It will also look at veiled forms of theological insight in his work through his understanding of otherness and the Nothing. It will be argued that these may aid our reflections on belief in God in the world today.

Radical thought

Since the Enlightenment we have come to think of the accumulation of knowledge as the human subject's mastery of the object. In the Sciences this object is the natural world and its processes. Arts disciplines take cultural phenomena and historical events as the object of their study. Yet the twentieth century saw a growing recognition that this rationalist process of observation was not the whole story. In both the Sciences (since Einstein and quantum theory) and the Arts (since the postmodern 'cultural turn') there has been a new emphasis on the subject's role in shaping the presentation and very nature of the object to be studied. Theology too has been profoundly affected by this radical extension of modernity's 'turn to the subject'. Yet theology goes even further to make the scandalous assertion that the object is not merely 'subject matter' but a causal agent in an irreducible process of self-revelation.

In Baudrillard's work we see the strong assertion of this theological principle as the era of modern enquiry and theory comes to an end. The object is not merely to be observed; the object itself is 'a strange attractor'.[2] In a sense, Baudrillard takes this theological principle of the 'self-revealing object' and applies it to all forms of inquiry including the sciences which, he believes, continue to labour under long-dead illusions:

> Science has never stopped churning out a reassuring scenario in which the world is being progressively deciphered by the advances of reason . . . But no one has ever advanced the hypothesis that things may discover us at the same time as we discover them, and that there is a dual relationship in discovery.[3]

In Baudrillard's account of radical thought in *The Perfect Crime*, the subject cannot sit above the object. He cannot even see himself as distinct from the object since this distinction is a fiction of which we can convince ourselves 'in the zone of perception' but which 'breaks down at the level of extreme and macroscopic phenomena'. It is this overarching perspective that restores 'the fundamental inseparability of the two, or in other words, the radical illusion of the world'.[4] This fusion of knower and known leading to a realization of the illusory nature of the objective world has strong mystical connotations which shall be explored further. But first we need to consider what kind of theology these new circumstances require and how Baudrillard's understanding of radical thought might open up new possibilities. Much contemporary theology remains within the paradigm of modern rationality that Baudrillard describes as 'banal thinking'. Scathingly, Baudrillard casts the acceptance of the constructs of reality (the Real) as 'one of the elementary forms of religious life. It is a failing of the understanding, a failing of common sense'. It is the 'last refuge of moral zealots and the apostles of rationality' and consequently the basis of 'otherworldly spiritual consolation'.[5] Although Baudrillard is not directly addressing the failings of theologians here, I see his criticisms as reflected in contemporary theology in two ways: first the enduring acceptance of natural/ supernatural, physical/metaphysical divide, and, second, the persistence of idealist, rationalistic modes of thought in much systematic theology. The former is unprepared fully to overhaul the modern, materialist worldview and continues to see God as external to the physical process of the world. It tends to reduce theology's focus to the Bible or the sacramental activity of the Church. The latter has trapped theology in a quasi-rationalistic discipline which analyses doctrine as if it were the laws of physics, perhaps in an attempt to justify its presence within an often hostile academy. The result in both cases is often the kind of banal thought that Baudrillard describes as 'maddeningly tedious and demoralizingly platitudinous'.[6]

Baudrillard would point us towards something more playful, more mysterious and less academically conventional. Baudrillard himself retired from the University of Nanterre in 1987 and held no subsequent academic post, preferring instead to work as an independent intellectual. As his writing became less theoretical and more fragmentary and performative, he lost much credibility within the academic community, while continuing to attract a growing international following. For him, radical thought now occurs, not in reasoned theorizing, but 'at the violent intersection of meaning and non-meaning, of truth and non-truth'.[7] Indeed it seems that radical thought is far more of a *being in* and *encountering* the world than a reading it. Radical thought 'must pride itself on not being an instrument of analysis, not being a critical tool'. Again he insists:

> Radical thought is a stranger to all resolving of the world in the direction of an objective reality and its deciphering. It does not

decipher. It anagrammatizes, it disperses concepts and ideas and, by its reversible sequencing, takes account both of meaning and of the fundamental illusoriness of meaning.[8]

Baudrillard's approach may seem like a nonsensical retreat into irrationality. And he would not entirely refute that! While he defends himself against charges of irresponsibility, nihilism and despair,[9] it is certainly the case that his account of radical thought is far more deconstructive than constructive. But this is his intention and it is this iconoclastic drive that makes his writing a powerful polemic against the temptation of thought to conform to prescribed systems and ideologies rather than challenge and destabilize them. Theology should destabilize patterns of thought and action in ways that unmask different forms of oppression and normalized violence. We need a theology of radical thought that does not conform to the dominant modes of thought, but is to be 'exceptional, anticipatory and at the margin'.[10] Nothing else has a hope of penetrating the totalized system of hyperreality.

It is for this reason that I think Baudrillard's radical thought is in fact far more akin to prayer than to rational theorizing. His aspiration is to a way of inhabiting the world that does not possess or dominate, does not break down and analyse, but embraces its otherness and discerns meaning in relation to it. It is reminiscent of D. H. Lawrence's poetic definition of thought as 'not a trick, or an exercise, or a set of dodges', but 'a man in his wholeness, wholly attending'.[11] Paradoxically this requires a certain kind of indifference to the world: 'The power of indifference, which is the quality of the mind, as opposed to the play of differences, which is the characteristic of the world'.[12] Indifference is not the same as apathy. But prayer is an antidote to the disposition that always approaches the world with domineering, objectifying intentions. Prayer cultivates a detachment so that the right kind of desiring for the world can begin to take shape. This is why Christians pray, 'Thy will be done'. So perhaps prayerful thought is the detached radical thought that replaces the acquisitive theorizing of modernity. Rather than seeking to have everything exhaustively assimilated into a system of understanding, 'We must reconcile nothing. We must keep open the otherness of forms, the disparity between terms; we must keep alive the forms of the irreducible'.[13]

From self to other

At the heart of all this is the rejection of a certain understanding of personhood. This is not merely the rational observer of post-Enlightenment enquiry. It is also, in a much broader sense, the autonomous human self that constitutes today's individualistic consumerism. To use the machine imagery that features strongly in Baudrillard's thought, human beings have been reduced to autonomous cells within the digital matrix of the hyperreal. Baudrillard sees this modern drift towards autonomy as rooted in the Christian inheritance of Western culture. Christianity encourages each of us to take full responsibility for our own lives. But this personal moral responsibility has been augmented 'with the help of the whole modern apparatus of information and communication' so that today autonomy has extended to every aspect of life:

> What this amounts to is an expulsion of the other, who has indeed become perfectly useless in the context of a programmed management of life, a regime where everything conspires to buttress the autarky of the individual cell. This, however, is an absurdity: no one can be expected to be entirely responsible for his own life . . . It is also a utopian notion.[14]

Baudrillard sees something quite inhuman in this isolated conception of existence. True life is symbolic exchange, a communion where our identity and desires are caught up in relationality:

> How much more human to place one's fate, one's desire and one's will in the hands of someone else. The result? A circulation of responsibility, a declination of wills, and a continual transferring of forms. Inasmuch as my life is played out within the other, it becomes a mystery to itself. Inasmuch as my will is transferred to the other, it too becomes a mystery to itself.[15]

Baudrillard's sense of otherness here is grounded in a symbolic exchange with other human beings but is not limited to it. As we have seen, all that is outside of oneself, the objective world, becomes the 'strange attractor'. It encompasses all 'otherness which erupts into our life, with stunning clarity, in the shape of a gesture, a face, a form, a word, a prophetic dream, a witticism, an object, a woman, or a desert'.[16] Baudrillard's otherness is a sacramental world to which we abandon our autonomous selfhood. This is what marks Baudrillard out from other thinkers who also identify a presence of otherness in the postmodern condition but insist on its 'absolute alterity', unchallenged by any notion of exchange. For Jacques Derrida, for example, not only is God 'wholly other' but 'every other (one) is every (bit) other' (*tout autre est tout autre*).[17] This leads to his rejection of symbolic exchange, as articulated by Mauss and so central to Baudrillard's thought. For Mauss (and hence for Baudrillard), it is the non-equivalence of the symbolic gift exchange that ruptures the value exchange of capitalism. Here the enormity of the gift (potlatch) is met by its reception and its return gift (the model of Chauvet's analysis of the Eucharist in Chapter 5) to establish a new symbolic relation that transcends economic logic. But for Derrida the irrationality of the exchange makes no odds: 'an exchanged gift is only a tit for tat, that is the annulment of the gift'[18] and so the economic logic continues. To him, a gift must always be entirely *aneconomic*. So it would seem that, for Derrida, exchange itself undermines radical otherness.

There is danger in making too much out of differing interpretations of Mauss here, since Derrida's use of otherness also seeks to be essentially ethical in taking 'responsibility' for others, fusing, in the biblical sense, the love of the Other that is God and the other that is neighbour. However, it may be said that Baudrillard's understanding of an otherness rooted in ritual (rather than economic) exchange is more intrinsically relational (and, in spite of himself, more conventionally Christian). He does not explicitly seek to establish this as a basis for ethical responsibility, but it may still point to a more Christian (even Trinitarian)[19] anthropology of identity bound up in *connectedness*. The oft quoted African proverb 'I am because we are' is perhaps an expression of the kind of understanding of human essence at stake here, one that has emerged in cultures more shaped by symbolic exchange than the post-Enlightenment West.

This is not a narrow discussion of anthropological and theological terms. The question is essentially whether or not the whole business of human exchange and sociality is somehow bound up with otherness and transcendence. This fault line has emerged in various areas of religious thought over recent years with a 'liberal' theology on the one hand emphasizing the cultural experience of faith and a 'post-liberal' theology on the other prioritizing divine revelation. It is through this dichotomy of the 'top-down' versus 'bottom-up' that many theological questions are framed today: Is the focus of religious life one of personal redemption or the building up of 'redeemed sociality'?[20] Should our focus be on *this* world or the world *to come*? Should religious communities prioritize a corporate unity or a doctrinal uniformity? These questions cut across the religious divides and relate in different ways to this issue of human relationality versus divine otherness. The two poles, communion and otherness, must clearly be held in some kind of tension, as many have argued.[21] But the tendency to overemphasize one or the other characterizes much theology today.

Baudrillard may seem like an unlikely contributor to these questions. It remains a matter of debate as to whether or not any transcendent otherness is truly detectable in his 'radical alterity'. Yet what we can say is that his concept of otherness does at least seem *irreducible*, reflecting a concept of grace, even in the givenness of life itself: 'I am not obliged to submit to something that does not depend on me – including my own existence. I am free of my birth – and in the same sense I can be free of my death'.[22] In his long journey from classical Marxism, this has become Baudrillard's strategy for overcoming alienation, not now 'the reappropriation of oneself – a tiresome process, without much prospect of success these days',[23] but almost the embracing of a yet deeper sense of alienation from self: 'This alternative path leads to an exponential defined elsewhere, virtually, in terms of total excentricity. It goes beyond alienation but in the same direction – to what is more other than the Other, to radical otherness'.[24]

As we have noted earlier, this combination of the denial of self and an abandonment both to dependence on others and to the 'strange attractor' (the essence of Baudrillard's entire approach) has profound mystical resonances. The mystical path is a journey into the utter transmutation of the self in God. Evelyn Underhill describes this as 'the stripping off of the I, the Me, the Mine, utter renouncement, or "self-naughting"' as an imperative to the unitive life. 'There is a final swallowing up of that wilful I-hood, that surface individuality which we ordinarily recognise as ourselves'.[25] Similarly, in his survey of the apophatic mystics Denys Turner sees something akin to Baudrillard's 'total excentricity' in the mystical dispossession that 'at once "decentres" us, for it disintegrates the experiential structures of selfhood on which, in experience, we centre ourselves, and at the same time draws into the divine love where we are "recentred" upon a ground beyond any possibility of experience'.[26] It is no longer us thinking God, but God thinking us. While Baudrillard would not speak of any kind of 'recentring', he talks about this kind of reversal in 'object thought'; 'thought become inhuman, is the form of thinking which actually comes to terms with impossible exchange. It no longer attempts to interpret the world, nor to exchange it for ideas . . . It becomes the world thinking us'.[27] It may be argued that Baudrillard's is a weak form of mysticism, more rooted in his strange metaphysics of the object than in a return to God. His own identification with mysticism[28] may be seen as ironic or glib. Yet perhaps we can see Baudrillard's identification of radical alterity in the immanent world as reawakening the possibilities for transcendence within a hyperreality that has seemingly become lost in nihilism and egotism.

God of nothing

Many will be reluctant to see these possibilities in Baudrillard when he declares himself to be a nihilist. But for him, it is not so much that he chooses not to believe as that in our present condition there is simply nothing to believe in (and this is surely the position many find themselves in today): 'Nihilism has been entirely realized no longer through destruction, but through simulation and deterrence'.[29] I would suggest that his embracing of the nihilism that surrounds him is not entirely ironic. The Real that has passed away is not to be lamented. He follows Nietzsche in holding that it was only ever a myth,[30] a creation of idealism, subjectivism, reason, positivism and science. Many other philosophers share Baudrillard's sense that this is simply the state of things today and that this need not necessarily be conceived as a counsel of despair. Gianni Vattimo sees our postmodern condition as characterized by a loss of centre, of objectivity, of supreme values and absolute principles. But such things have invariably been associated with dominant power, particularly in their religious forms. So, Vattimo hopes, 'the Babel of postmodernity, the end of metaphysics, the dissolution of Being, and nihilism are not just expressions of our historical limitations,

but also of our specific calling'.[31] He argues that nihilism is not
the enemy of faith but rather 'the (most likely, probable) form
of religiosity of our epoch',[32] an opportunity to experience the
reduction of the religious to its essence, in the case of Christianity,
Christ's call to love. We might say that this sweeping away of the
human constructs of modernity presents a new opportunity to
encounter God.

The possibilities of this kind of nihilism are only enigmatically
present in Baudrillard. Yet he has a similar kind of excitement
as Vattimo about the *tabula rasa* we are faced with at the end of
modernity. In an interview with Sylvère Lotringer he states that, 'We
can't avoid going a long way with negativity, with nihilism and all.
But then don't you think a more exciting world opens up? Not a
more reassuring world, but certainly more thrilling'.[33] Similarly, he
has written, 'For me, I will always have an empty, perfectly non-
functional and therefore free space where I can express my thoughts.
Once the machine has exhausted all of its functions, I slip into
what is left, without trying to judge or condemn it. And maybe a
new space-time domain for thought is now opening?'[34] A passage
in *Impossible Exchange* explores this potential of 'the Nothing' of
nihilism as the opposite to the positivism of the real and of value.
Baudrillard describes this Nothing in explicitly theological terms. It
is 'the underlying fabric of all things, it is safely there for eternity'.[35]

> The Nothing is the only ground – or background – against
> which we can apprehend existence. It is existence's potential of
> absence and nullity, but also of energy (there is an analogy here
> with the quantum void). In this sense, things only ever exist *ex
> nihilo*. Things only ever exist out of nothing. The Nothing does
> not cease to exist as soon as there is something. The Nothing
> continues (not) to exist just beneath the surface of things. This is
> Macedonio Fernández's 'perpetual continuation of the Nothing'.
> Everything which exists continues, then, not to exist at the same
> time. This antinomy is beyond the imagining of our critical
> understanding.[36]

Parallels with Vattimo's understanding of nihilism are reinforced
in passages from *Symbolic Exchange and Death* where the
Nothing is brought about by poetry as the mode of language that
'exterminates the name of God'. 'Enjoyment proceeds from the

death of God and his name, and more generally from the fact that where something used to be – a name, a signfier, an agency – *nothing remains*.[37]

It may be too simplistic to say here that the Nothing is Baudrillard's nihilistic account of the divine presence. In any event, he believes, 'it profits us "nothing" to concern ourselves overmuch either with it or with the apparent hegemony of an objective world'.[38] Nonetheless, this may be read as a radically non-positivist theology that has strong parallels with the mystical tradition. Baudrillard's language of nihilism is particularly reminiscent of John of the Cross' abandonment of self into 'nothing' since God is nothing (i.e. no thing). Similar to Baudrillard's radical thought, John of the Cross calls for a dispossession of much that is thought necessary to human knowledge and morality, including value and virtue: 'To arrive at being all, desire to be nothing. To come to the knowledge of all, desire the knowledge of nothing'.[39] More likely to have been of direct influence on Baudrillard is Nietzsche's characterization of Christianity in *The Anti-christ* as the placing of the emphasis of life '*on nothingness*'.[40] For Nietzsche, the Christian God has always been the deification of nothing and his followers seekers after nothing. So while Baudrillard's wider criticisms of Christianity are very much in line with Nietzsche, it may be that, in his rejection of Nietzsche's emphasis on the human and his 'will to power', Baudrillard goes to a deeper nihilism that is the mystical foundation of belief and is a basis even for hope.[41] In the eradication of both reason and of the stable human subject it supposes, locating ourselves in the Nothing and surrendering our control over the world may, paradoxically, open up a new perspective:

> Rather than humanity bringing reason into a chaotic universe, it would be the bringing of disorder . . . which constitutes an extraordinary *coup de force*: establishing a point (even a simulated one) outside the universe from which to see and reflect (on) the universe.[42]

Theological hyperreality

We seem to glimpse here the possibility of theology. But how might we do theology in such a world and where might we conceive of God's action within it? Baudrillard observes (more clearly than many theologians) how much Western theism was linked with the modern rationalistic order. God's raison d'être was 'to guarantee, to bless certain causal connections, allowing him to make a last judgment on the world, piercing through, at certain places, the fog that obscures his luminous gaze upon chaos'.[43] Such understandings of God have been strong in European thought, particularly since the eighteenth century when Archdeacon Paley saw the marks of design in the universe as evidence for a designer, just as a mechanical watch gives evidence of a watchmaker. But Baudrillard insists that this rationalistic order has passed away and an irrational hyperreality has replaced modernity's stable causal system. In this less certain age, Baudrillard suggests, 'It's no surprise that God has died, leaving behind a perfectly free and random world, and leaving the task of organizing things to a blind divinity named Chance'.[44]

In the place of Enlightenment order is the overdetermined world of codified hyperreality. As we have seen, what is of interest to Baudrillard in this system is what challenges and unsettles the dominant logic of digitality and the virtual. Chance and indeterminacy, risk and coincidence can all generate singularity and meaning. What is of interest lies outside of the causal system. Baudrillard proposes a theology where God has arranged things 'so that what happens without reason, what arrives through an extremely rare and unlikely probability, is more meaningful than what happens as a result of a cause. What happens accidentally takes on a meaning and intensity that we no longer assign to rational occurrence'.[45]

At times Baudrillard even implies in these singular moments of meaning and intensity a pattern that he describes as 'destiny', a world so arranged that 'nothing but coincidences' occur.[46] While not a theory of providence rooted in a conventional understanding of God, this destiny stems from his central theme of the reversibility of subject and object. Indeed, this is the 'principle of reversibility in action' – that we are not in control of our lives in the way we might think: 'I would say that it is the world which thinks us – not discursively, but the wrong way round, against all our efforts to think *it* the right way round'.[47] He emphatically denies a religious sense of predestination here but nonetheless maintains that there are moments that reveal the 'complicity between things', when 'such a moment is predestined for a particular other, such a word for another one, as in a poem where you have the impression that the words were always preordained to meet'.[48]

All of this points to a far subtler understanding of divine action than is commonly elucidated. On the one hand it implies the rejection of a kind of theological realism that locates the divine within the order of being. Baudrillard warns us against a God who is conceived as the guarantor of the causal system. The critiques of Martin Heidegger and subsequent theologians such as Jean-Luc Marion have shown us how these 'ontotheologies' have been profoundly anthropocentric, inevitably reducing the divine. On the other hand we need to resist the theological anti-realism which has essentially abandoned any theological account of the physical world and reduced God to a metaphor or (following Feuerbach) a projection of human aspiration. Both accounts fail to overcome modernity's reductionist account of the Real.

In embracing Baudrillard's rejection of modernity's conceptions of reality, today's theology must engage with a *realism beyond the real*, seeking to identify God within the singularities and events that disrupt the self-referentiality of the virtual. In a sense, our reappraisal of what we are prepared to count as real calls for a theological hyperreality. This would be an understanding of the Real that goes beyond the post-Enlightenment parameters with its dualistic separation of physical and metaphysical. We need an account of the Real more open to the presence and activity of God and a theological enterprise that sees us more actively engaged in the cultivation of those revelatory moments. John Caputo describes his theological project as 'a magnifying *hyper-realism of the event*, of the event stirring in the name of God with all the hyperbolic action of the beyond, of the force that commands my attention and demands that I collaborate in its realization, in transforming it into existence'.[49]

This book has sought to point in the direction of such a hyperreal theological approach. In Chapter 5 we considered an understanding of selfhood grounded, not in modernity's individualistic autonomy, but in the relationality of symbolic ritual and ceremony. In Chapter 6 we sought to conceive of time, not in the conventional linear sense, but in terms of the patterning of singularities that generate meaningful narrative. In Chapter 7 we explored an account of Good and Evil that calls into question the optimistic view of progress and expansion that has dominated the Western mindset in the capitalist era. In Chapter 8 we sought to move beyond the contemporary impasses on gender and sex through a more fluid understanding of identity constituted by self-giving. In Chapter 9 we reappraised theory and systematic thought itself through a new appreciation of fragment and poetry. And now we have ventured to speculate whether the sweeping away of so much of what was considered real is not the terrifying annihilation of theology but the possibility of a new dawn in which the divine might be perceived as the true reality that overcomes the Real.

In all these areas we have sought to look beyond much of the conventional thinking that the Western tradition of thought has passed down to us to consider these questions in the light of God and within the less certain categories and parameters of our age. In so doing I have taken Baudrillard into theological territory he would not himself have walked. But in his nomadic desert wanderings he is an undoubtedly insightful companion to those seeking meaningful theological insight in today's world.

NOTES

Introduction

1 *Cool Memories V*, 56.
2 M. Guillaume & J. Baudrillard, *Radical Alterity*, 2008, 13.
3 *America*, 63.
4 Interview with Caroline Bayard and Graham Knight, published in *Research in Semiotic Inquiry/Recherches Semiotiques*, Vol. 16, No. 1–2, Spring 1996.
5 Interview with Sylvère Lotringer, *Forget Foucault* (Los Angeles: Semiotext(e), 2007), 85.
6 *Simulation and Simulacra*, 229.
7 Paul Janz, *The Command of Grace* (London: T&T Clark, 2009), 2.
8 Ibid., 3.
9 *Impossible Exchange*, 22.
10 Richard Sennett, *The Culture of the New Capitalism* (New Haven: Yale University Press, 2006), 11–12.
11 Robert Skidelsky, *Keynes: The Return of the Master* (London: Penguin, 2009), xvii.
12 Douglas Kellner, 'Jean Baudrillard', *The Stanford Encyclopedia of Philosophy (Winter 2009 Edition)*, Edward N. Zalta (ed.).
13 Nicholas Zurbrugg, *Critical Vices: The Myths of Postmodern Theory* (Amsterdam: G + B Arts International, 2000), 80.
14 Wachowski Brothers, Time Warner, 1999.
15 Interview with Brett Staples, 'Editorial Observer; A French Philosopher Talks Back to Hollywood and "The Matrix"'. The New York Times Late Edition: Final , Section A , Page 24 , Column 1, p. 788 May 24th, 2002.
16 Nicholas Zurbrugg, *Critical Vices: The Myths of Postmodern Theory* (Amsterdam: G + B Arts International, 2000), 83.
17 *The Spirit of Terrorism*, 41. The *New York Times Book Review* suggested he deserved 'first prize for cerebral coldbloodedness'.

18 Baudrillard's reputation has been so damaged in many circles by his comments on 9/11 that it is worth quoting his defence: 'I do not praise murderous attacks—that would be idiotic. Terrorism is not a contemporary form of revolution against oppression and capitalism. No ideology, no struggle for an objective, not even Islamic fundamentalism, can explain it. . . .I have glorified nothing, accused nobody, justified nothing. One should not confuse the messenger with his message. I have endeavoured to analyze the process through which the unbounded expansion of globalization creates the conditions for its own destruction'. Cited in Douglas Kellner, 'Jean Baudrillard', *The Stanford Encyclopedia of Philosophy (Winter 2009 Edition)*, Edward N. Zalta (ed.).

Chapter 1

1 *For a Critique of the Political Economy of the Sign*, 163.

2 Among the popular surveys, neither Gary Gutting's *French Philosophy in the Twentieth Century* (Cambridge: CUP, 2001) nor Alan Shrift's *Twentieth-Century French Philosophy: Key Themes and Thinkers* (Oxford: Blackwell, 2006) nor Eric Matthew's *Twentieth-Century French Philosophy* (Oxford: OUP, 1996) contain more than a passing reference to Baudrillard. He is a particularly sad omission from Shrift's *Nietzsche's French Legacy* (London: Routledge, 1995). *The Columbia History of Twentieth-Century French Thought* (edited by Lawrence Kritzman; New York: Columbia University Press, 2006) does, however, contain a substantial article (415–18) reflecting Baudrillard's greater prominence in the United States.

3 Baudrillard first started to publish in Sartre's journal, *Les Temps modernes*.

4 Baudrillard restates this Saussurean principle in his final years: 'We think we advance by way of ideas – that is the fantasy of every theorist, every philosopher – but it is also words themselves which generate or regenerate ideas, which act as "shifters". At those moments, ideas intersect, intermingle at the level of the word. And the word then serves as an operator – but a non-technical operator – in a catalysis in which language itself is in play. Which makes it at least as important a stake in the game as ideas'. *Passwords*, x.

5 Gary Gutting, *French Philosophy in the Twentieth Century* (Cambridge: CUP, 2001), 222.

6 Mike Gane, *Baudrillard: Critical and Fatal Theory* (London: Routledge, 1991), 29. Published as *Conversations with Claude Lévis-Strauss*, ed. Georges Charbonnier (trans. John and Doreen Weightman; London: Jonathan Cape, 1969).

7 Ibid., 5.

8 *Passwords*, 17.

9 Julia Kristeva, *Revolution in Poetic Language* (New York: Columbia University Press, 1984).

10 Roland Barthes, *Mythologies* (London: Vintage, 2000), 140.

11 Henri Lefebvre, *Critique of Everyday Life*, Vol. 1 (London: Verso, 2008), 4.

12 Ibid., 97.

13 Richard J. Lane, *Jean Baudrillard* (London: Routledge, 2000), 4.

14 Macedonio Fernandez (1874–1952) and Elias Canetti (1905–1994) are two other important examples.

15 This form of primarily nation-based capitalism is a largely European phenomenon. The economies of developing countries were far more dependent on imperial trade links throughout the twentieth century and remain more dependent on exports, unable to rely on their own internal markets.

16 See Weber's discussion of capital accounting in Section II:13, 'The Formal and Substantive Rationality of a Money Economy' in *The Theory of Social and Economic Organization* (New York: The Free Press of Glencoe, 1947). Weber sees this rationalizing process as heavily constructed from the beginning: 'This rationality is of a purely formal character. No matter what the standards of value by which they are measured, the requirements of formal and of substantive rationality are always in principle in conflict, no matter how numerous the individual cases in which they may coincide empirically' (212).

17 Many on the Left, following Marx himself, would argue that rather than meeting the demands of just reward for labour, the interventions of the democratic socialist state have in many ways 'obscured' such demands, providing the tokenistic appearance of redistribution while perpetuating the subordination of workers to employers.

18 Scott Lash and John Urry, *The End of Organized Capitalism* (Cambridge: Polity, 1987).

19 A useful illustration of this acceleration of the global economy is measure of global direct foreign investment (DFI, the amount of

capital invested in an enterprise by foreign investors). Between 1970 and 1980 DFI increased by 310%, between 1980 and 1990 it increased by 277% and between 1990 and 2000 it increased by 572%. The overall increase for this 30-year period was over a 100-fold. What was true of capital was also true of commodities. In the UK, for example, foreign commodity imports increased by 177% in the two decades from 1980 to 2000 while British exports increased by 141% – statistics taken from United Nations Conference on Trade and Development.

20 *System of Objects*, 218.
21 Guy Debord, *Society of the Spectacle* (trans. Ken Knabb, Eastbourne: Soul Bay Press, 2009), 24.
22 Ibid., 27
23 Ibid., 30–31.
24 See *Capital* (Oxford: Oxford University Press, 1995), especially Part I, Chapters 2–3 and Part II. This very premise is complicated for Baudrillard since it presupposes that the labourer is the owner of his own labour power, whereas for Baudrillard the concept of the individual is itself a product of the general system of exchange.
25 *For a Critique of the Political Economy of the Sign*, 71.
26 Ibid., 139.
27 See Roland Barthes, *Mythologies* (trans. A. Lavers; London: Vintage 1993). Baudrillard deconstructs Barthes' whole analysis of denotation and connotation since, he contends, the idea of denotation is based on the needs of objectivity (a direct relation of the signifier to a precise reality). Baudrillard views denotation as nothing more than the most attractive and subtle connotation.
28 *For a Critique of the Political Economy of the Sign*, 147.
29 *The Consumer Society*, 25.
30 *The Mirror of Production* (St Louis: Telos Press, 1975).
31 *For a Critique of the Political Economy of the Sign*, 122.
32 *The Consumer Society*, 79.
33 Douglas Kellner, *Jean Baudrillard: From Marxism to Postmodernism and Beyond* (Cambridge: Polity Press, 1989), 215.
34 Ibid.
35 *The Consumer Society*, 82–3. Another Baudrillard commentator, Zygmunt Bauman, has taken up this theme to demonstrate how, in the advanced capitalist economy, consumption has replaced work and work-associated membership as the core principle governing our identity, 'The same central role which was played by work,

by job, occupation, profession, in modern society, is now performed in contemporary society by consumer choice', *Freedom* (Oxford: Oxford University Press, 1988).

36 *For a Critique of the Political Economy of the Sign*, 65.

Chapter 2

1   *America*, 32.
2   *The Consumer Society*, 190.
3   Herbert Marcuse, *One-Dimensional Man: Studies in the Ideology of Advanced Industrial Society* (London: Routledge Classics, 1992).
4   Michel Foucault, *The History of Sexuality: The Will to Knowledge Vol. I* (London: Penguin, 1998).
5   *The Consumer Society*, 191.
6   *Symbolic Exchange and Death*, 8.
7   *Simulacra and Simulation*, 6. Baudrillard's use of the term 'sacrament' here reflects some of the ambivalences in its Christian usage. The Greek word, from which it derives, μυστηριον, originates from the Hellenistic world in the vocabulary of the mystery cults to associate it with initiation into *sophia*. Its New Testament usage at times retains the connotation of a divine *secret* concerning God's benevolent plan for the world (Ephesians 1:9). However, other texts suggest that its referent is clear, and is no longer destined, as in pagan mysteries, to be hidden. On the contrary, it should be publicly preached (Romans 16:25ff) and is henceforth made visible even to the Gentiles since the mystery is 'Christ in you' (Colossians 1:29).
8   Ibid., 50.
9   Ibid.
10 Ibid., 51.
11 Ibid.
12 Ibid., 54.
13 Ibid.
14 Ibid., 57.
15 *Simulacra and Simulation*, 6.
16 Walter Benjamin, *The Work of Art in the Age of Mechanical Reproduction* (trans. J. A. Underwood; London: Penguin, 2008).
17 Marshall McLuhan, *Understanding Media: the Extensions of Man* (London: Routledge, 2001).
18 *Symbolic Exchange and Death*, 56.

19 Ibid., 65.
20 *For a Critique of the Political Economy of the Sign*, 61.
21 *Simulacra and Simulation*, 12.
22 Ibid.
23 Ibid., 12–13.
24 Ibid., 13.
25 Douglas Kellner, *Jean Baudrillard: From Marxism to Postmodernism and Beyond* (Cambridge: Polity Press, 1989), 107. Paul Hegarty contradicts Kellner, arguing, 'Baudrillard would presumably not dispute the dominance of capital, but, for him, this "dominance" is in a form that differs widely from Kellner's view'. Baudrillard argues that 'capitalism is no longer the possession of "capitalists", and that capital is itself a term that becomes highly unstable in a world of notional money and where the increase in technologization means that the workforce is not doubly oppressed, but is increasingly pointless, whether in terms of a "maintenance" of capital or a "revolution of the proletariat"'. *Jean Baudrillard: Live Theory* (London: Continuum, 2004), 40. It should be noted here that Baudrillard's analysis is specific to the developed world (particularly those parts of it that have radically embraced the consumer model of capitalism). Part of the reason for the 'dematerialization' of production has been the exportation of exploitative labour to 'under-developed' countries that have yet to enter this 'era of simulation' in which the Western world currently finds itself. However, as consumer ideology is increasingly globalized as part of the free-market liberal democracy model, the impact of pseudo-liberation through consumer freedom is sure to spread.
26 *America*, 80.
27 Simon Blackburn, 'Au Revoir Baudrillard', *Prospect Magazine*, 29th April 2007, Issue 133.
28 *Symbolic Exchange and Death*, 57.
29 Quoted in *Symbolic Exchange and Death*, 57.
30 Ibid., 59.
31 *Symbolic Exchange and Death*, 59–60.
32 Ibid., 61–2.
33 Ibid., 64.
34 Ibid., 65.
35 Ibid., 66.
36 *Symbolic Exchange and Death*, 66–7.
37 *In the Shadow of the Silent Majorities*, 35.

38 Ibid., 37.
39 Ibid., 43.
40 Ibid., 47.
41 Ibid., 68.
42 Ibid., 66–7.
43 Ibid., 37.
44 Ibid., 74.
45 Ibid., 37.
46 Ibid., 75.
47 *Simulacra and Simulation*, 4.
48 Ibid.
49 Ibid. 5.
50 *In the Shadow of the Silent Majorities*, 39.
51 Ibid., 35.
52 Ludwig Feuerbach, *The Essence of Christianity* (trans. G. Elliot; New York: Prometheus Books, 1989), xix. Baudrillard similarly characterizes the nineteenth century as 'the radical destruction of appearances, the disenchantment of the world and its abandonment to the violence of interpretation and of history' (*Simulacra and Simulation*, 160). It would seem that this 'radical destruction of appearances' is precisely the eradication of the religion that Baudrillard believes to have long been reduced to the cynical manipulation of signs. Feuerbach certainly played a key role in this process.
53 Feuerbach, *The Essence of Christianity* (trans. G. Elliot; New York: Prometheus Books, 1989), xix.
54 T. M. Gouldstone The Rise and Decline of Anglican Idealism in the Nineteenth Century, (Basingstoke: Palgrave MacMillan, 2005), 192.
55 Slavoj Žižek, *Welcome to the Desert of the Real* (London: Verso, 2002), 69–70.
56 Johann Baptist Metz, 'For a renewed Church before a New Council: a Concept in Four Theses' in *Toward Vatican III*, eds. David Tracy, Hans Kung and Johann Baptist Metz (New York: Seabury Press, 1978), 143.

Chapter 3

1 *Forget Foucault & Forget Baudrillard, an interview with Sylvère Lotringer*, 84.
2 *Passwords*, 77.

3 *The Intelligence of Evil or The Lucidity Pact*, 128.

4 *Simulacra and Simulation*, 159.

5 The extent to which Baudrillard's prophecy about the dominance of the virtual has become a reality is difficult to measure but successive studies are demonstrating this shift, particularly among younger people. Research by consultancy K Zero.co.uk in 2009 showed 579 million people participate in virtual worlds such as Second Life in which you inhabit your own avatar. This had grown by 39% in just the second quarter of that year. Poptropica.com, a virtual world aimed at 5- to 10-year olds, had 76 million registered users. Research by the University of Cambridge Engineering Design Centre revealed that one in five Britons spends more than seven hours a day using communication technologies. One-third said they felt 'overwhelmed' by technology.

6 *Screened Out*, 179.

7 *System of Objects*, 223.

8 *Fatal Strategies*, 111.

9 Ibid., 113–4.

10 At the core of Hegel's dialectic is what he terms the 'negation of the negation'. For Hegel, truths only function within a wider context in which for things to be determinate is for them to negate what they are not.

11 The first explicit acknowledgement I can find of this shift is in industrial designer Brooks Stevens who coined the phrase 'planned obsolescence' in his work *Industrial Strength* (1954). See Glenn Adamson, *Industrial Strength Design: How Brooks Stevens Shaped Your World* (Cambridge, Mass.: MIT Press, 2003).

12 For example, Lord Haskins' report for the Department for the Environment, Food and Rural Affairs in 2005 showed that one-third of food grown for consumption in the UK is thrown away.

13 *The Consumer Society*, 43

14 Ibid., 47. 'Potlatch' is a ceremonial giving away or destruction of property to enhance prestige, practiced by some North American Indian peoples. Baudrillard's debt to Marcel Mauss in his account of the potlatch will be discussed later.

15 Rex Butler summarizes Baudrillard's position, 'It is exactly through imposing restrictions on the possible satisfaction of wants, in maintaining the distinction between classes, in making certain forms of consumption dangerous or anti-social, that taxation works to

make consumption meaningful . . . not only does taxation maintain existing needs and the distinctions between classes, but it makes them possible from the very beginning'. *Jean Baudrillard: The Defence of the Real* (London: Sage 1999), 51.

16 A slogan of Prime Minister Jacques Chaban-Delmas (1969–72). For the distinctive political context of this period in French history; see Rod Kedward, *La vie en bleu: France and the French since 1900* (London: Penguin, 2005), Chapter 17.

17 See Tanzi & Schuknecht, *Public Spending in the 20th Century: A Global Perspective* (Cambridge: CUP, 2000), 18ff.

18 *The Consumer Society*, 38. See also Slavoj Žižek's view of global capitalism as the totality equating to the dialectical unity of itself and of its other in *Welcome to the Desert of the Real* (London: Verso, 2002), 51.

19 Ibid., 161.

20 *The Intelligence of Evil or the Lucidity Pact*, 17.

21 Ibid., 133.

22 *Forget Baudrillard*, 88.

23 *Passwords*, 15.

24 *Symbolic Exchange and Death*, 1.

25 Jacques Derrida's contention on this point is discussed in Chapter 10.

26 Marcel Mauss, *The Gift: The Form and Reason for Exchange in Archaic Societies* (trans. W. D. Halls; London: Routledge, 1990), 39.

27 Ibid., 42.

28 Georges Bataille, *Visions of Excess: Selected Writings, 1927–39* (trans. Stoekl, Lovitt & Leslie; Minneapolis: University of Minnesota Press, 1985), 121.

29 *For a Critique of the Political Economy of the Sign*, 64.

30 Ibid., 66.

31 *Symbolic Exchange and Death*, 126.

32 Ibid., 183.

33 Ibid., 131.

34 Ibid.

35 Ibid., 132

36 Jacques Derrida, *The Gift of Death* (trans. David Wills; Chicago: University of Chicago Press, 1995), 45.

37 Richard Lane (*Jean Baudrillard,* London: Routledge, 2000) points out that Baudrillard himself, in his early writing, states: 'Alluding to primitive societies is undoubtedly dangerous'. It could be that

Baudrillard is saying that the use of such allusions to primitive societies is dangerous in the way in which it undermines Western thought and the foundations of capitalism. But Lane suggests that in acknowledging the dangers of alluding to primitive societies, Baudrillard recognizes that these allusions themselves reveal 'a more complex and potentially destabilizing world beneath or behind the concept of potlatch' (55). Drawing on the work of Chris Bracken in *The Potlatch Papers* (1997), he suggests that there is an indeterminacy in the term 'potlatch' which even Mauss sidesteps 'by deciding that it is a conceptual word that is more accurate in terms of the abstracted processes of potlatching than in the cultures and languages from which this abstraction is in part derived' (53). Baudrillard, perhaps from the start, works with a simulacrum of primitivism.

38 *The Consumer Society*, 67.
39 *Fatal Strategies*, 81.
40 Ibid., 99.
41 *Passwords*, 21.
42 *Seduction*, 7.
43 *Passwords*, 24. I put 'evil' in inverted commas here because of the ambivalent (almost ironic) sense in which Baudrillard uses it, discussed further in Chapter 7.
44 *Forget Baudrillard*, 91.
45 Douglas Kellner contends that 'Baudrillard's aristocratic values and vision of human beings here reproduces the discourses of a conservative-individualist tradition to which he now attaches himself', *Jean Baudrillard: From Marxism to Postmodernism and Beyond* (Cambridge: Polity Press, 1989) 195.
46 *Forget Baudrillard*, 89.

Chapter 4

1 *Cool Memories*, 4.
2 *Impossible Exchange*, 131.
3 Ibid., 5.
4 Ibid., 4.
5 Ibid., 6.
6 Ibid., 4.
7 Ibid., 5.

8   Ibid., 6.
9   Ibid., 7.
10 Ibid.
11 Ibid.
12 Ibid., 13.
13 Ibid., 13–14.
14 William Pawlett, *Jean Baudrillard* (London: Routledge, 2007), 126.
15 Rowan Williams, *Ethics, Economics and Global Justice*, a lecture to the Welsh Centre for International Affairs, Cardiff, 7 March 2009.
16 *Impossible Exchange*, 14.
17 *The Intelligence of Evil or the Lucidity Pact*, 122.
18 Ibid.
19 *The Gulf War Did Not Take Place*, 62.
20 Ibid., 23.
21 Ibid., 27.
22 Ibid., 63.
23 Slavoj Žižek, *Welcome to the Desert of the Real* (London: Verso, 2002), 37.
24 See, for example, Susan Sontag who accuses Baudrillard of 'breathtaking provincialism', *Regarding the Pain of Others* (London: Penguin Books, 2003), 98.
25 *The Gulf War Did Not Take Place*, 64.
26 *The Consumer Society*, 174.
27 Ibid., 177.
28 *The Intelligence of Evil or the Lucidity Pact*, 126.
29 *The Consumer Society*, 189.
30 *The Transparency of Evil*, 44–5.
31 *Radical Alterity*, 41.
32 Ibid., 43.
33 Ibid., 78.
34 Rowan Williams, *Lost Icons: Reflections on Cultural Bereavement* (Edinburgh: T&T Clark, 2000), 9.

Chapter 5

1   *The Transparency of Evil*, 144.
2   Henri Lefebvre, *Critique of Everyday Life*, Vol. 1 (London: Verso, 2008), 216.
3   Ibid., 222.

4 *In the Shadow of the Silent Majorities*, 39.
5 E.g. David Ford and Daniel Hardy argue that 'praising God, recognizing him as God in feeling, word and action, is a key to the ecology in which right knowledge of God grows', *Living in Praise: Worshipping and Knowing God* (London: Darton, Longman and Todd, 2005), 141. From a more philosophical perspective, Catherine Pickstock argues for a restoration of liturgical order over the metaphysics of modernity, *After Writing: On The Liturgical Consummation of Philosophy* (Oxford: Blackwell, 1998). Taking up themes explored by Stanley Hauerwas and William Cavanaugh, Bernd Wannenwetsch explores the political dimensions of the worship of the Church as a basis for Christian Ethics, *Political Worship* (Oxford: OUP, 2009).
6 *For a Critique of the Political Economy of the Sign*, 65.
7 Herbert Marcuse, *One-Dimensional Man: Studies in the Ideology of Advanced Industrial Society* (London: Routledge Classics), 59.
8 E.g. Dorothy A. Lee's work on *The Symbolic Narratives of the Fourth Gospel* (Sheffield: Journal for the Study of the New Testament Supplement Series 95, 1994).
9 Paul Avis, *God and the Creative Imagination: Metaphor, symbol and myth in religion and theology* (London: Routledge, 1999), 106.
10 Louis-Marie Chauvet, *Symbole et sacrament. Une relecture sacrementalle de l'existence chrétienne* (coll. Cogitatio fidei, 144, Paris: Les Éditions du Cerf, 1987), 104–5. My translation.
11 See Marcel Mauss, *The Gift: The Form and Reason for Exchange in Archaic Societies* (trans. W. D. Halls; London: Routledge, 1990).
12 *Passwords*, 17.
13 Louis-Marie Chauvet, *Symbole et sacrament. Une relecture sacrementalle de l'existence chrétienne* (coll. Cogitatio fidei, 144, Paris: Les Éditions du Cerf, 1987), 128. My translation.
14 Ibid., 113. My translation.
15 Ibid., 273. My translation.
16 see René Girard, *Violence and the Sacred* (London: Continuum, 2005).
17 Louis-Marie Chauvet, *Symbole et sacrament. Une relecture sacrementalle de l'existence chrétienne* (coll. Cogitatio fidei, 144, Paris: Les Éditions du Cerf, 1987), 318. My translation.
18 This is found in a modified form in the Church of England's *Common Worship* as Eucharistic Prayer B.

19 Louis-Marie Chauvet, *Symbole et sacrament. Une relecture sacrementalle de l'existence chrétienne* (coll. Cogitatio fidei, 144, Paris: Les Éditions du Cerf, 1987), 282. My translation.

20 While the anaphoras of Basil and Chrysostom emphasize the offering of praise and thanksgiving, Chauvet sees this more paradoxical anamnesis of offering the gifts themselves back to God expressed in the anaphora of Hippolytus and in the anaphoras of the forth and fifth centuries. Common Worship prefers 'As we offer you this our sacrifice of praise and thanksgiving, we bring before you this bread and this cup . . . '.

21 Louis-Marie Chauvet, *Symbole et sacrament. Une relecture sacrementalle de l'existence chrétienne* (coll. Cogitatio fidei, 144, Paris: Les Éditions du Cerf, 1987), 284. My translation.

22 Ibid., 274. My translation.

23 *Fatal Strategies*, 166ff.

24 See also Louis-Marie Chauvet, 'The Broken Bread as Theological figure', in *Sacramental Presence in a Post-Modern Context*, eds. L. Boeve and L. Leijssen (Leuven: Leuven University Press, 2001).

25 *Symbolic Exchange and Death*, 133.

26 In Baudrillard's view, baptism does nothing more than define the moral event of birth. Immortality – an imaginary concept of the Church – grew alongside the segregation of the dead. Originally only the distinctive emblem of power (such as that of the Pharaohs in Egyptian religion), the immortality of the soul acts throughout Christianity as an egalitarian myth, as a democratic beyond as opposed to worldly inequality before death. Baudrillard insists that this is only a myth and that immortality has in fact been granted sparingly as a means of control. Throughout the history of the Church, he argues, primitive peoples, women, children, madmen and criminals have rarely been accorded this status. Suppression of the dead has therefore been about the assertion of power: 'Power is only possible if death is no longer free, only if the dead are put under surveillance, in anticipation of the confinement of life in its entirety . . . we know that sacerdotal power is based on a monopoly over death and exclusive control over relations with the dead' (130). Much can be said in response to Baudrillard's critique. Christopher Rowland, in *Political Theology*, eds. Scott & Cavanaugh (London: Blackwells, 2004), for example, argues that the Pauline ethic 'There is neither Jew nor Greek, slave nor free, male nor female' (Galatians

3:28) was central to the political constitution of the *ekklesia* in the first four centuries of Christianity. Nonetheless, Baudrillard does at least raise the important point that the doctrine of the immortality of the soul has been far from consistent from the early years of Christianity, also discussed by Christopher Rowland, *Christian Origins* (Cambridge: SPCK, 1985), 92. The dangers of dualism stressed by Baudrillard are also the subject of much current discussion among theologians and discussed further in Chapter 6.

27 Romans 6.4.
28 *Fatal Strategies*, 166.
29 Ibid., 167.
30 Ibid., 168.
31 Ibid., 168.
32 *Passwords*, 17.
33 See Michel Foucault, *The Order of Things* (London: Routledge Classics, 2001).
34 *Fatal Strategies*, 168.
35 Ibid., 151.
36 Ibid., 153.
37 Ibid., 166.
38 Ibid., 172.
39 In Jean-Luc Marion, *The Crossing of the Visible* (Stanford: Stanford University Press, 2004), 46–65.
40 Jean-Luc Marion, *The Crossing of the Visible* (Stanford: Stanford University Press, 2004), 51.
41 *Screened Out* (trans. Chris Turner; London: Verso, 2002).
42 Jean-Luc Marion, *The Crossing of the Visible* (Stanford: Stanford University Press, 2004), 54.
43 Ibid.
44 Ibid., 57.
45 Ibid., 58.
46 Ibid., 64.
47 Ibid., 65. This approach of a semiotic political theology for the hyperreal age is not without its critics. Paul Ricoeur is among those who express concern that a total rejection of the metaphysics of being would 'disenculture' Judeo-Christian theology and result in their marginalization. Conversely, however, in answer to his question, 'would a theology of love that sets out to do without ontology be in a better position to conclude a new pact with western reason?' he does at least see possibilities for a more solid inculturation (André LaCocque

and Paul Ricoeur, *Thinking Biblically: Exegetical and Hermeneutical Studies* (Chicago: University of Chicago Press, 1998), 359).

48 *Impossible Exchange*, 130.
49 Ibid., 134.
50 *Fatal Strategies*, 151.
51 *Impossible Exchange*, 131.
52 Ibid., 131.

Chapter 6

1 *The Gulf War did not take place*, 49.
2 *Passwords*, 66.
3 Ibid., 61.
4 *The Agony of Power*, 72.
5 G. E. Wright, *God Who Acts: Biblical Theology as Recital* (London: SCM Press, 1952), 116–7
6 *America*, 80.
7 Ibid., 76.
8 *The Gulf War never Happened*.
9 *The Illusion of the End*, 1.
10 Ibid., 3.
11 Francis Fukuyama, *The End of History and the Last man* (London: Hamish Hamilton, 1992).
12 *The Illusion of the End*, 4.
13 Ibid., 32.
14 Ibid., 11.
15 Ibid., 32.
16 Ibid., 116.
17 Ibid., 4.
18 Ibid., 91.
19 Ibid., 95.
20 Ibid., 9.
21 *Symbolic Exchange and Death*, 178.
22 *The Illusion of the End*, 7.
23 Revelation 21.
24 *The Illusion of the End*, 7.
25 Ibid., 8.
26 The first 11 books in this series sold over 40 million copies making Tim LaHaye and Jerry B Jenkins America's best selling novelists.

27 *Life in 2050: Amazing Science, Familiar Threats,* Pew Research
    Center For The People and The Press based in Washington DC. An
    Associated Press poll in 1997 had this figure at 24%.
28 *The Illusion of the End,* 8.
29 See Glenn W. Shuck, *Marks of the Beast: The Left Behind Novels
    and the Struggle for Evangelical Identity* (New York: New York
    University Press, 2005).
30 Origen, *De Principiis* in Roberts and Donaldson (eds.), *Ante Nicene
    Fathers,* Vol IV (Peabody, Mass.: Hendrickson Publishers, 2004),
    385ff.
31 *The Illusion of the End,* 90.
32 Ibid., 95–6.
33 Ibid., 8.
34 *Symbolic Exchange and Death,* 40.
35 Ibid., 37.
36 Ibid., 36.
37 'The Violence of the Global', in *The Spirit of Terrorism,* 97.
38 Ibid.
39 Ibid., 104.
40 Ibid., 105.
41 *The Agony of Power,* 67.
42 Ibid.
43 *Symbolic Exchange and Death,* 39.
44 Acts 6:8.
45 *The Illusion of the End,* 21.
46 *The Agony of Power,* 112–13.
47 *Passwords,* 74.
48 'The Violence of the Global', in *The Spirit of Terrorism,* 96.
49 *Passwords,* 74.
50 e.g. Matthew 11:25 and Ephesians 6:18.
51 Antonio Negri, *Time for Revolution* (London: Continuum, 2003),
    155.
52 *The Agony of Power,* 75.

Chapter 7

1 *The Intelligence of Evil of the Lucidity Pact,* 146.
2 Ibid., 159.

3 Friedrich Nietzsche, *Beyond Good and Evil* (London: Penguin Classics, 2003).
4 *The Transparency of Evil*, 85.
5 *The Agony of Power*, 87.
6 *The Intelligence of Evil of the Lucidity Pact*, 146.
7 Max Weber, *The Spirit of Capitalism* (London: Routledge Classics, 2001).
8 *The Intelligence of Evil of the Lucidity Pact*, 146.
9 Friedrich Nietzsche, *The Gay Science* (Cambridge: CUP, 2001), 120.
10 *The Agony of Power*, 85.
11 Ibid., 88.
12 Ibid., 110.
13 Ibid.
14 *The Transparency of Evil*, 106.
15 E.g. SARS in 2003, Avian flu in 2005 and Swine flu in 2009.
16 *The Agony of Power*, 95.
17 Ibid., 97.
18 *The Transparency of Evil*, 82.
19 Ibid., 107.
20 *The Agony of Power*, 111.
21 President Reagan's speech to the National Association of Evangelicals, in Orlando, Florida, on 8th March 1983.
22 *The Agony of Power*, 111–2.
23 Jason Burke argues that al-Qaeda is 'a messy and rough designation' and that 'labelling opponents "al-Qaeda" allows repressive governments to do what they want with limited international criticism' *Al-Qaeda: The True Story of Radical Islam* (London: Penguin, 2007), 1, 15.
24 Isaiah 5.20.
25 *The Transparency of Evil*, 82.
26 E.g. the women's religious movement known as the Beguines was outlawed in a decree of the Council of Vienne in 1312, one of many such groups perceived as heretical at this time.
27 *The Transparency of Evil*, 107.
28 Ibid., 107.
29 *Forget Baudrillard*, 116.
30 *Passwords*, 35.
31 Ibid., 29.
32 *The Transparency of Evil*, 105.

33 'Secret report: biofuel caused food crisis', *The Guardian*, 3 July 2008.
34 *Passwords*, 29–30.
35 Ibid., 35.
36 Ibid., 35.
37 Michael Novak, *The Spirit of Democratic Capitalism* (New York: Madison Books, 1991), 336.
38 *The Consumer Society*, 42.
39 Ibid., 52.
40 Ibid.
41 Martha Nussbaum argues that 'increase in GDP is not very well correlated with increase in average household income, particularly in a world of globalization, where profits may be repatriated by foreign investors without contributing to the spending power of a country's citizens'. *Creating Capabilities: The Human Development Approach* (Cambridge, Mass.: Harvard University Press, 2011), 48.
42 Roland Barthes, *Mythologies* (trans. A. Lavers; London: Vintage, 1993), 141.
43 Ibid., 143.
44 E.g. Joseph Stiglitz, Amartya Sen & Jean-Paul Fitoussi, *Mis-Measuring Our Lives: Why GDP Doesn't Add Up*, The Report by the Commission on the Measurement of Economic Performance and Social Progress (New York: The New Press, 2010).
45 *The Consumer Society*, 40.
46 See, for example, David Cameron's address to the Zeitgeist Europe conference in May 2006. Benedict XVI has also begun to question the 'activist' culture, quoting Bernard of Clairvaux that 'much work often leads to hardness of heart' (Sunday Angelus, 20 August 2006).
47 Alain Badiou, *Saint Paul: The Foundation of Universalism* (Stanford University Press, 2003), 5.
48 Ibid., 14. Nonetheless, for Badiou this founding 'truth' still designates 'a mere fable' (6).
49 *The Spirit of Terrorism*, 92.
50 Ibid, 89–90.
51 See the *Enough Project* strategy paper: http://www.enoughproject.org/publications/comprehensive-approach-conflict-minerals-strategy-paper.
52 *The Intelligence of Evil of the Lucidity Pact*, 129.
53 See 'The Ideology of the World Market' in Hardt & Negri, *Empire* (Cambridge Mass.: Harvard University Press, 2000). While this work is a strong polemic against market ideology, the authors concede that 'trade brings differences together' (150). 'The world market

establishes a real politics of difference' (151) since, in marketing terms, 'every difference is an opportunity' (152).

54 'The Violence of the Global', in *The Spirit of Terrorism*, 97.

55 William Cavanaugh, *Being Consumed: Economics and Christian Desire* (Michigan: Wm. B. Eerdmans, 2008), 70–1.

56 Ibid., 76.

Chapter 8

1 *America*, 34.

2 *The Consumer Society*, 129.

3 Although significantly Bishop John Robinson was one of the chief 'witnesses for the defence' in the Lady Chatterly trial.

4 *The Consumer Society*, 129.

5 Ibid., 132.

6 Ibid., 133.

7 *The Consumer Society*, 133.

8 Ibid.

9 Mark Poster, 'Swan's Way: Care of Self in the Hyperreal', in *Baudrillard Now: Current Perspectives in Baudrillard Studies* (Cambridge: Polity Press, 2009), 96.

10 *Symbolic Exchange and Death*, 101.

11 Ibid., 116.

12 Ibid., 104.

13 Germain Greer, *The Whole Woman* (London: Transworld Publishers, 1999), 27ff.

14 William Pawlett, *Jean Baudrillard* (London: Routledge, 2007), 98.

15 *For a Critique of the Political Economy of the Sign*, 99.

16 Douglas Kellner, *Jean Baudrillard: From Marxism to Postmodernism and Beyond* (Cambridge: Polity Press, 1989).

17 *Seduction*, 19.

18 Ibid., 21.

19 Germain Greer writes, 'The female sector is disappearing as women are inducted into a neutered workforce. Though these processes were well advanced when *The Female Eunuch* was written, it was a year or two later that I found myself arguing for the recovery of women's culture' *The Whole Woman* (London: Transworld Publishers, 1999), 323.

20 *Seduction*, 14.

21 Originally printed in Liberation. Reprinted in *Screened Out*, 9ff.
22 *Screened Out*, 9.
23 Ibid., 11.
24 *Screened Out*, 10.
25 Ibid., 13. Baudrillard uses the metaphor of an 'orgy' to refer to the sexual and social experimentation of the feminist and homosexual liberation movements of the 1960s and 1970s.
26 *Symbolic Exchange and Death*, 107.
27 Graham Ward in Milbank, Pickstock & Ward, *Radical Orthodoxy*, (London: Routledge, 1999), 170.
28 Ibid. 171.
29 Timothy Radcliffe, *What's the Point of Being a Christian?* (London: Continuum, 2005), 93.
30 Ibid., 95.
31 William Pawlett, *Jean Baudrillard* (London: Routledge, 2007), 97.
32 Galatians 3.28.
33 *Radical Alterity*, 60.
34 Ibid.
35 Rowan Williams, *The Body's Grace* (Michael Harding Memorial Address), (London: Lesbian and Gay Christian Movement, 1989). The phrase 'the body's grace' is taken from *The Day of the Scorpion* in Paul Scott's *Raj Quartet*.

Chapter 9

1 *The Intelligence of Evil or the Lucidity Pact*, 27.
2 Marshall McLuhan, *Understanding Media* (London: Abacus, 1973).
3 *The Perfect Crime*, 104.
4 Adeel et al., *Re-thinking Policies to Cope with Desertification* (United Nations University, 2007).
5 *Cool Memories V*, 33.
6 *America*, 71.
7 Ibid., 100.
8 Ibid., 99.
9 Michel De Certeau, *The Mystical Fable, Vol. 1: The Sixteenth and Seventeenth Centuries*, trans. Michael B. Smith (Chicago: University of Chicago Press, 1992), 293.
10 *America*, 124.

11 Simon Schama has similarly argued that rather than viewing landscapes as purely material fact, we should consider how they are 'culture before they are nature; constructs of the imagination projected onto wood and water and rock', *Landscape and Memory* (London: HarperCollins, 1995), 61.

12 *America*, 127.

13 Ibid., 68–9.

14 Denys Turner, *The Darkness of God: Negativity in Christian Mysticism* (Cambridge: CUP, 1995).

15 David Jasper, *The Sacred Desert: Religion, Literature, Art, and Culture*, Oxford: Blackwells, 2004, 52.

16 In his entry on Baudrillard in the Stanford Encyclopedia of Philosophy, Douglas Kellner suggests, somewhat dismissively, that Baudrillard's later work is 'of more literary interest'. 'Jean Baudrillard', *The Stanford Encyclopedia of Philosophy (Winter 2009 Edition)*, Edward N. Zalta (ed.).

17 *Fragments*, 22.

18 Ibid., 26–7.

19 *Fragments: Cool Memories III, 1990–95*, 8.

20 David Shields, *Reality Hunger: A Manifesto* (London: Hamish Hamilton, 2010), 3.

21 Vivian Gornick, *The Situation and the Story*, quoted in David Shields, *Reality Hunger: A Manifesto* (London: Hamish Hamilton, 2010), 22.

22 *Transparency of Evil*, 39–40.

23 *Fragments: Cool Memories III, 1990–95*, 8.

24 John D'Agata, *The Next American Essay*, quoted in David Shields, *Reality Hunger: A Manifesto* (London: Hamish Hamilton, 2010), 28.

25 *Cool Memories V*, 31.

26 Laurence Freeman's introduction to Rowan Williams, Where God Happens: Discovering Christ in One Another (Boston: New Seeds Books, 2005), 1–2.

27 *Cool Memories V*, 17.

28 David Tracy, 'Fragments: The Spirituality of Our Times', in Caputo, J. (ed.), *God, the Gift and Postmodernism* (Bloomington: Indiana University Press, 1999), 170.

29 Ibid., 171.

30 Ibid., 173.

31 Ibid., 179.

32 Jacques Derrida's response to David Tracy, 'Fragments: The Spirituality of Our Times', in Caputo, J. (ed.), *God, the Gift and Postmodernism* (Bloomington: Indiana University Press, 1999), 181ff.

33 Indeed Baudrillard's strategy all along has been to destabilize totality by drawing attention to the fragment, the remnant, the marginalized other, be that the female over the male, the evil over the good, the nothing over the something, illusion over truth.

34 Published under the title *The Stucco Angel* in 1978.

35 Published in *The Uncollected Baudrillard*, 84. The poem's use in *Seduction* (61–2) is identified by Richard G. Smith in *The Baudrillard Dictionary* (Edinburgh: Edinburgh University Press, 2010).

36 *Seduction*, 62.

37 *Symbolic Exchange and Death*, 198.

38 Ibid., 205.

39 Ibid., 209.

40 Ibid., 199.

41 Cf. Acts 17.23.

42 Jean-Luc Marion, 'Chapter 3' *God Without Being* (trans. Thomas A. Carlson; Chicago: University of Chicago Press, 1991).

43 See René Girard, *Violence and the Sacred* (London: Continuum, 2005).

44 Jean-Luc Marion, *God Without Being* (trans. Thomas A. Carlson; Chicago: University of Chicago Press, 1991), 71.

45 Paul S. Fiddes, *Freedom and Limit: A Dialogue Between Literature and Christian Doctrine* (London: MacMillan, 1991), 10.

46 *The Perfect Crime*, 105.

47 Paul S. Fiddes, *Freedom and Limit: A Dialogue Between Literature and Christian Doctrine* (London: MacMillan, 1991), 10.

48 Proverbs 30.18–19.

49 *The Transparency of Evil*, 3.

50 Paul Ricoeur, *The Symbol of Evil* (trans. E. Buchanan; New York: Harper & Row, 1967).

51 Paul S. Fiddes, *Freedom and Limit: A Dialogue Between Literature and Christian Doctrine* (London: MacMillan, 1991), 11.

52 A selection of Baudrillard's photographs was published in *Photographies 1985–98* (Neue Galerie Graz: Hatje Cantz Publishers, 1999).

53 Mike Gane, *Baudrillard: Critical and Fatal Theory*, (London: Routledge, 1991), 42.

Chapter 10

1   *The Transparency of Evil*, 168.
2   Ibid., 172.
3   *Impossible Exchange*, 22.
4   *The Perfect Crime*, 54.
5   Ibid., 95–6.
6   *The Perfect Crime*, 103.
7   Ibid., 96.
8   Ibid., 105.
9   Ibid., 104.
10 *The Perfect Crime*, 101.
11 From the poem 'Thought' in D. H. Lawrence, *Complete Poems*, ed. Vivian de Sola Pinto and Warren Roberts (Harmondsworth: Penguin Books, 1993), 673.
12 *The Perfect Crime*, 103.
13 Ibid., 123.
14 *The Transparency of Evil*, 165.
15 Ibid., 165–6.
16 Ibid., 174.
17 Jacques Derrida, *The Gift of Death* (Chicago: University of Chicago Press, 1995), 82ff.
18 Jacques Derrida, *Given Time: I. Counterfeit Money* (Chicago: University of Chicago Press, 1992), 37.
19 In his discussion of John Milbank's theology of Gift, which has parallels to both Baudrillard and Chauvet, I think Todd Billings is right to urge caution in use of 'anthropological language from the gift-giving discussion to describe a trinitarian soteriology of the "gift" – but with insufficient conditioning of these concepts though biblical exegesis and inadequate apophatic modesty'(100). But the debate is nonetheless insightful. Todd J. Billings, 'John Milbank's Theology of the "Gift" and Calvin's Theology of Grace: A Critical Comparison', Modern Theology (21:1, January 2005), 87–105.
20 Daniel W. Hardy, *God's Ways with the World: Thinking and Practising Christian Faith* (Edinburgh: T&T Clark, 1996), Chapter 11.
21 e.g. John D. Zizoulas, *Communion and Otherness* (London: Continuum, 2006).
22 *The Transparency of Evil*, 168.
23 Ibid., 173.

24 Ibid., 173.
25 Evelyn Underhill, *Mysticism: The Nature and Development of Spiritual Consciousness* (Oxford: One World, 1993), 425.
26 Denys Turner, *The Darkness of God: Negativity in Christian Mysticism* (Cambridge: Cambridge University Press, 1995), 251.
27 *Impossible Exchange*, 24.
28 As cited in the opening chapter. Interview with Caroline Bayard and Graham Knight, published in *Research in Semiotic Inquiry/ Recherches semiotiques*, Vol. 16, No. 1–2, Spring 1996.
29 Simulacra and Simulation, 159.
30 Friedrich Nietzsche, *Twilight of the Idols* (London: Penguin Classics, 1990), 50–1.
31 Gianni Vattimo in Caputo and Scanlon (eds.), *Transcendence and Beyond: A Postmodern Inquiry* (Bloomington: Indiana University Press, 2007), 48.
32 Ibid., 47.
33 *Forget Baudrillard*, 74.
34 *The Agony of Power*, 127.
35 *Impossible Exchange*, 11.
36 Ibid., 8–9. Macedonio Fernandez (1874–1952) was an avant-garde Argentinian writer and philosopher. The work of his student Jorge Luis Borges is also often quoted by Baudrillard.
37 *Symbolic Exchange and Death*, 209.
38 *Impossible Exchange*, 11.
39 John of the Cross, 'The Ascent of Mount Carmel', 13:11 in *John of the Cross: Selected Writings* (ed. Kieran Kavanaugh, New Jersey: Paulist Press, 1987), 78.
40 Friedrich Nietzsche, *The Anti-Christ, Ecce Homo, Twilight of the Idols, and Other Writings* (ed. Aaron Ridley; Cambridge: Cambridge University Press, 2005), 39.
41 Thomas Altizer sees this as the paradox already present in Nietzsche that the death of Jesus prefigures his own 'death of God' as 'giving birth to a pure and total nihilism, the most devastatingly destructive nihilism in history, but one which is revealed as such only in the death of the uniquely Christian God. That death not only reveals our nihilism, but enacts it, and enacts it as a finally redemptive event'. So Altizer (also drawing on Dostoyevsky) interprets Nietzsche's nihilism in a similar way to Vattimo, as offering the potential for a restoration of religion to its core reality. Thomas J. J. Altizer, *The Contemporary Jesus* (New York: State University of New York Press, 1997), 159.

42 *Impossible Exchange*, 25.
43 *Fatal Strategies*, 149.
44 Ibid.
45 Ibid.
46 *Passwords*, 73.
47 Ibid.
48 Ibid., 74.
49 John Caputo *The Weakness of God: A Theology of the Event* (Bloomington: Indiana University Press, 2006), 123.

BIBLIOGRAPHY

Works by Baudrillard

The System of Objects (trans. James Benedict; London: Verso, 1996). First original language publication 1968.

For a Critique of the Political Economy of the Sign (trans. Charles Levin; New York: Telos Press, 1981). First original language publication 1972.

The Consumer Society (trans. Chris Turner; London: Sage, 1998). First original language publication 1970.

The Mirror of Production (trans. Mark Poster; St Louis: Telos Press, 1975). First original language publication 1973.

Symbolic Exchange and Death (trans. Iain Hamilton Grant; London: Sage, 1993). First original language publication 1976.

Forget Foucault & Forget Baudrillard, an Interview with Sylvère Lotringer (New York: Semiotext(e), 1987). First original language publication 1977.

In the Shadow of the Silent Majorities (trans. Paul Foss et al.; Los Angeles: Semiotext(e), 2007). First original language publication 1978.

Seduction (trans. Brian Singer; New York: St. Martin Press, 1990). First original language publication 1979.

Simulacra and Simulation (trans. Sheila Faria Glaser; Michigan: University of Michigan Press, 1994). First original language publication 1981.

Fatal Strategies (trans. Philip Beitchman and W. G. J. Niesluchowski; London: Pluto Press, 1999. First original language publication 1983.

The Illusion of the End (trans. Chris Turner; Cambridge: Polity Press, 1994). First original language publication 1992.

America (trans. Chris Turner; London: Verso, 1988). First original language publication 1986.

Cool Memories (trans. Chris Turner; London: Verso, 1990). First original language publication 1987.

The Transparency of Evil (trans. James Benedict; London: Verso, 1993). First original language publication 1990.

The Perfect Crime (trans. Chris Turner; London: Verso, 2008). First original language publication 1995.

Fragments: Cool Memories III, 1990–1995 (trans. Emily Agar; London: Verso, 2007). First original language publication 1993.

The Gulf War Did Not Take Place (trans. Paul Patton; Sydney: Power Publications, 1995). First original language publication 1991.

Radical Alterity (with Marc Guillaume, trans. Ames Hodges; Los Angeles: Semiotext(e), 2008). First original language publication 1994 and 1998.

Impossible Exchange (trans. Chris Turner; London Verso, 2001). First original language publication 1999.

Photographies 1985–1998 (Neue Galerie Graz: Hatje Cantz Publishers, 1999).

Screened Out (trans. Chris Turner; London: Verso, 2002). First original language publication 2000.

The Uncollected Baudrillard (ed. Gary Genosko; London: Sage, 2001)

Passwords (trans. Chris Turner; London: Verso, 2003). First original language publication 2000.

Cool Memories IV (trans. Chris Turner; London: Verso, 2003). First original language publication 2000.

Fragments (trans. Chris Turner; London: Routledge, 2004). First original language publication 2001.

The Spirit of Terrorism (trans. Chris Turner; London: Verso, 2002). First original language publication 2002 (*Power Inferno,* including *The Violence of the Global*, published separately in the same year).

The Intelligence of Evil or The Lucidity Pact (trans. Chris Turner; Oxford: Berg, 2007). First original language publication 2004.

Exiles From Dialogue, with Enrique Valiente Noailles (trans. Chris Turner; Cambridge: Polity, 2007). First original language publication 2005.

Cool Memories V (trans. Chris Turner; Cambridge: Polity, 2006). First original language publication 2005.

The Agony of Power, (trans. Ames Hodges; Los Angeles: Semiotext(e), 2010). First original language publication 2007.

Other works

Adamson, Glenn, *Industrial Strength Design: How Brooks Stevens Shaped Your World* (Cambridge, MA: MIT Press, 2003).

Adeel, Zafar et al., *Re-thinking Policies to Cope with Desertification* (Hamilton, ON: United Nations University, 2007).

Altizer, Thomas J. J., *The Contemporary Jesus* (New York: State University of New York Press, 1997).

Avis, Paul, *God and the Creative Imagination: Metaphor, Symbol and Myth in Religion and Theology* (London: Routledge, 1999).

Badiou, Alain, *Saint Paul: The Foundation of Universalism* (Stanford, CA: Stanford University Press, 2003).

Barthes, Roland, *Elements of Semiology* (New York: Hill and Wang, 1967).

—, *Mythologies* (trans. A. Lavers; London: Vintage 1993).

Bataille, Georges, *Visions of Excess: Selected Writings, 1927–1939* (trans. Stoekl, Lovitt & Leslie; Minneapolis, MN: University of Minnesota Press, 1985).

Bauman, Zygmunt, *Freedom* (Oxford: Oxford University Press, 1988).

Benjamin, Walter, *The Work of Art in the Age of Mechanical Reproduction* (trans. J. A. Underwood; London: Penguin, 2008).

Billings, J. Todd, 'John Milbank's Theology of "Gift" and Calvin's Theology of Grace: A Critical Comparison', *Modern Theology* (21:1, January 2005).

Burke, Jason, *Al-Qaeda: The True Story of Radical Islam* (London: Penguin, 2007).

Butler, Rex, *Jean Baudrillard: The Defence of the Real* (London: Sage 1999).

Caputo, John D., *The Weakness of God: A Theology of the Event* (Bloomington, IN: Indiana University Press, 2006).

Caputo, John D., & Scanlon, Michael J., *God, the Gift and Postmodernism* (Bloomington, IN: Indiana University Press, 1999).

Caputo, John D., & Scanlon, Michael J. (eds.), *Transcendence and Beyond: A Postmodern Inquiry* (Bloomington, IN: Indiana University Press, 2007).

Caputo, John D., & Vattimo, Gianni, *After the Death of God* (New York: Columbia University Press, 2007).

Cavanaugh, William, *Being Consumed: Economics and Christian Desire* (Michigan: Wm. B. Eerdmans, 2008).

Certeau, Michel de, *The Mystical Fable, Vol. 1: The Sixteenth and Seventeenth Centuries*, trans. Michael B. Smith (Chicago, IL: University of Chicago Press, 1992).

Charbonnier, Georges (ed.), *Conversations with Claude Lévi-Strauss* (trans. John and Doreen Weightman; London: Jonathan Cape, 1969).

Chauvet, Louis-Marie, *Symbole et sacrament. Une relecture sacramentalle de l'existence chrétienne* (coll. Cogitatio fidei, 144, Paris: Les Éditions du Cerf, 1987).

—, 'The Broken Bread as Theological Figure', in *Sacramental Presence in the Post-Modern Context,* eds. Lieven Boeve, & Lambert Leijssen (Leuven: Leuven University Press, 2001).

Debord, Guy, *Society of the Spectacle* (trans. Ken Knabb, Eastbourne: Soul Bay Press, 2009).

Derrida, Jacques, *Given Time: I. Counterfeit Money* (trans. Peggy Kamuf; Chicago, IL: University of Chicago Press, 1992).

—, *The Gift of Death* (trans. David Wills; Chicago, IL: University of Chicago Press, 1995).

Eagleton, Terry, *After Theory* (London: Penguin, 2003).

Feuerbach, Ludwig, *The Essence of Christianity* (trans. G. Elliot; New York: Prometheus Books, 1989).

Fiddes, Paul S., *Freedom and Limit: A Dialogue Between Literature and Christian Doctrine* (London: MacMillan, 1991).

Ford, David F., & Hardy, Daniel W., *Living in Praise: Worshipping and Knowing God* (London: Darton, Longman and Todd, 2005).

Foucault, Michel, *The History of Sexuality: The Will to Knowledge, Vol. I* (London: Penguin, 1998).

—, *The Order of Things* (London: Routledge Classics, 2001).

Fukuyama, Francis, *The End of History and the Last Man* (London: Hamish Hamilton, 1992).

Gabriel, Yiannis, & Lang, Tim, *The Unmanageable Consumer: Contemporary Consumption and its Fragmentations* (London: Sage Publications, 1995).

Gane, Mike, *Baudrillard: Critical and Fatal Theory*, (London: Routledge, 1991).

Gauthier, Alain, *Baudrillard: Une Pensée Singulière* (Paris: Nouvelles Éditions Lignes, 2008).

Girard, René, *Violence and the Sacred* (London: Continuum, 2005).

Gouldstone, Timothy M., *The Rise and Decline of Anglican Idealism in the Nineteenth Century* (Basingstoke: Palgrave MacMillan, 2005).

Greer, Germain, *The Whole Woman* (London: Transworld Publishers, 1999).

Gutting, Gary, *French Philosophy in the Twentieth Century* (Cambridge: Cambridge University Press, 2001).

—, *Thinking the Impossible: French Philosophy Since 1960* (Oxford: Oxford University Press, 2011).

Hardt, Michael, & Negri, Antonio, *Empire* (Cambridge MA: Harvard University Press, 2000).

Hardy, Daniel W., *God's Ways with the World: Thinking and Practising Christian Faith* (Edinburgh: T&T Clark, 1996).

Hegarty, Paul, *Jean Baudrillard: Live Theory* (London: Continuum, 2004).

Hughes, Graham, *Worship as Meaning: A Liturgical Theology for Late Modernity* (Cambridge: Cambridge University Press, 2003).

Janz, Paul, *The Command of Grace* (London: T&T Clark, 2009).

Jasper, David, *The Sacred Desert: Religion, Literature, Art, and Culture* (Oxford: Blackwells, 2004).

John of the Cross, *John of the Cross: Selected Writings* (ed. Kieran Kavanaugh; New Jersey: Paulist Press, 1987).

Kedward, Rod, *La vie en bleu: France and the French since 1900* (London: Penguin, 2005).

Kellner, Douglas, *Jean Baudrillard: From Marxism to Postmodernism and Beyond* (Cambridge: Polity Press, 1989).

—, 'Jean Baudrillard', *The Stanford Encyclopedia of Philosophy (Winter 2009 Edition)*, Edward N. Zalta (ed.).

Kristeva, Julia, *Revolution in Poetic Language* (New York: Columbia University Press, 1984).

Kritzman, Lawrence D. (ed.), *The Columbia History of Twentieth-Century French Thought* (New York: Columbia University Press, 2006).

LaCocque, André and Ricoeur, Paul, *Thinking Biblically: Exegetical and Hermeneutical Studies* (Chicago, IL: University of Chicago Press, 1998).

Lane, Richard J., *Jean Baudrillard* (London: Routledge, 2000).

Lash, Scott, and Urry, John, *The End of Organised Capitalism* (Cambridge: Polity, 1987).

—, *Economies of Signs and Space* (London: Sage 1994).

Lawrence, David H., *Complete Poems*, eds. Vivian de Sola Pinto, & Warren Roberts (Harmondsworth: Penguin Books, 1993).

Lee, Dorothy A., *The Symbolic Narratives of the Fourth Gospel: The Interplay of Form and Meaning* (Sheffield: Journal for the Study of the New Testament Supplement Series 95, 1994).

Lefebvre, Henri, *Critique of Everyday Life, Vol. 1* (London: Verso, 2008).

Leonelli, Ludovic, *La Séduction Baudrillard* (Paris: École nationale supérieure des beaux-arts, 2007).

Marcuse, Herbert, *One-Dimensional Man: Studies in the Ideology of Advanced Industrial Society* (London: Routledge Classics, 1992).

Marion, Jean-Luc, *God Without Being* (trans. Thomas A. Carlson; Chicago, IL: University of Chicago Press, 1991).

—, *The Crossing of the Visible* (trans. James K.A. Smith; Stanford, CA: Stanford University Press, 2004).

Marx, Karl, *Capital* (Oxford: Oxford University Press, 1995).

Matthews, Eric, *Twentieth Century French Philosophy* (Oxford: Oxford University Press, 1996).

Mauss, Marcel, *The Gift: The Form and Reason for Exchange in Archaic Societies*, (trans. W. D. Halls; London: Routledge, 1990).

McLuhan, Marshall, *Understanding Media: the Extensions of Man* (London: Routledge, 2001).

Metz, Johann B., 'For a renewed Church before a New Council: a Concept in Four Theses' in *Toward Vatican III*, eds. David Tracy,

Hans Kung, & Johann Baptist Metz (New York: Seabury Press, 1978).

Negri, Antonio, *Time for Revolution* (London: Continuum, 2003).

Nietzsche, Friedrich, *Twilight of the Idols* (London: Penguin Classics, 1990).

—, *The Gay Science* (Cambridge: Cambridge University Press, 2001).

—, *Beyond Good and Evil* (London: Penguin Classics, 2003).

—, *The Anti-Christ, Ecce Homo, Twilight of the Idols, and Other Writings* (ed. Aaron Ridley; Cambridge: Cambridge University Press, 2005).

Novak, Michael, *The Spirit of Democratic Capitalism* (New York: Madison Books, 1991).

Nussbaum, Martha, *Creating Capabilities: The Human Development Approach* (Cambridge, MA: Harvard University Press, 2011).

Origen, '*De Principiis*' in *Ante Nicene Fathers, Vol IV*, eds. Alexander Roberts, & James Donaldson (Peabody, MA: Hendrickson Publishers, 2004).

Pawlett, William, *Jean Baudrillard* (London: Routledge, 2007).

Pickstock, Catherine, *After Writing: On The Liturgical Consummation of Philosophy* (Oxford: Blackwell, 1998).

Poster, Mark, 'Swan's Way: Care of Self in the Hyperreal', in *Baudrillard Now: Current Perspectives in Baudrillard Studies*, ed. R. Bishop (Cambridge: Polity Press, 2009).

Radcliffe, Timothy, *What's the Point of Being a Christian?* (London: Continuum, 2005).

Ricoeur, Paul, *The Symbol of Evil* (trans. E. Buchanan; New York: Harper & Row, 1967).

Rojek, Chris, & Turner, Bryan, *Forget Baudrillard?* (London: Routledge, 1993).

Rowland, Christopher, *Christian Origins* (Cambridge: SPCK, 1985).

Schama, Simon, *Landscape and Memory* (London: HarperCollins, 1995).

Schrift, Alan D., *Nietzsche's French Legacy: A Genealogy of Poststructuralism* (London: Routledge, 1995).

—, *Twentieth-Century French Philosophy: Key Themes and Thinkers* (Oxford: Blackwells, 2006).

Scott, Peter, & Cavanaugh, William (eds.), *Political Theology* (London: Blackwells, 2004).

Sennett, Richard, *The Culture of the New Capitalism* (New Haven: Yale University Press, 2006).

Shields, David, *Reality Hunger: A Manifesto* (London: Hamish Hamilton, 2010).

Shuck, Glenn W., *Marks of the Beast: The Left Behind Novels and the Struggle for Evangelical Identity* (New York: New York University Press, 2005).

Skidelsky, Robert, *Keynes: The Return of the Master* (London: Penguin, 2009).

Smith, Richard G. (ed.), *The Baudrillard Dictionary* (Edinburgh: Edinburgh University Press, 2010).

Sontag, Susan, *Regarding the Pain of Others*, (London: Penguin books, 2003).

Stiglitz, Joseph, Sen, Amartya, & Fitoussi, Jean-Paul, *Mis-Measuring Our Lives: Why GDP Doesn't Add Up*, The Report by the Commission on the Measurement of Economic Performance and Social Progress (New York: The New Press, 2010).

Tanzi, Vito, & Schuknecht, Ludger, *Public Spending in the 20th Century: A Global Perspective*, (Cambridge: Cambridge University Press, 2000).

Tracy, David, 'Fragments: The Spirituality of Our Times', in Caputo, J. (ed.), *God, the Gift and Postmodernism* (Bloomington, IN: Indiana University Press, 1999).

Turner, Denys, *The Darkness of God: Negativity in Christian Mysticism* (Cambridge: Cambridge University Press, 1995).

Wannenwetsch, Bernd, *Political Worship* (Oxford: Oxford University Press, 2009).

Ward, Graham, in Milbank, Pickstock & Ward, *Radical Orthodoxy* (London: Routledge, 1999).

Weber, Max, *The Theory of Social and Economic Organisation* (New York: The Free Press of Glencoe, 1947).

—, *The Spirit of Capitalism* (London: Routledge Classics, 2001).

Wilden, Anthony, *System and Structure: Essays in Communication and Exchange* (London: Tavistock, 1972).

Williams, Rowan, *The Body's Grace, Michael Harding Memorial Address* (London: Lesbian and Gay Christian Movement, 1989).

—, *Lost Icons: Reflections on Cultural Bereavement* (Edinburgh: T&T Clark, 2000).

—, *On Christian Theology* (Oxford: Blackwell, 2000).

—, *Where God Happens: Discovering Christ in One Another* (Boston: New Seed Books, 2005).

—, *Ethics, Economics and Global Justice*, a Lecture to the Welsh Centre for International Affairs, Cardiff, 7 March 2009.

Wright, George E., *God Who Acts: Biblical Theology as Recital* (London: SCM Press, 1952).

Žižek, Slavoj, *Welcome to the Desert of the Real* (London: Verso, 2002).

Zizoulas, John D., *Communion and Otherness* (London: Continuum, 2006).

INDEX

alienation   17, 26–7, 67, 138
alterity and otherness   62–3
anthropology
   Lévi-Strauss   13–14
   symbolic exchange   47
Aquinas, Thomas
   Summa Theologica   120
autonomous selfhood   136

banal thinking   134
barring body
   Basquiat, Jean-Michel   110
   female body   111
   Phallus Exchange
      Standard   110–11
   signs, media
      representations   110
Barthes, Roland
   myth   101–2
   Mythologies
      clothes   16
   traditional opulent wedding
      functions   17
   sign exchange-value   23
Basquiat, Jean-Michel   110
Benjamin, Walter
   *The Work of Art in the
      Age of Mechanical
      Reproduction*   29
Bracken, Chris
   The Potlatch Papers   154n. 37

capitalist economy
   consumer society   20–1

criticisms   24–5
liberty   25
Marxism
   facets, political Left   18–19
   organized industrial
      period   19–20
Cavanaugh, William   104–5
ceremony
   cultivation of social
      relation   73–4
   eschatological dimension   76–7
   interchangeability of form   75
   modernity's denial of
      death   74–5
   resisting functionality and over-
      determinism   75–6
Chauvet, Louis-Marie   70–3
The Consumer Society   17, 43,
   50, 61
Cosmetic Surgery   108

Debord, Guy
   electoral participation   34
   Society of the Spectacle   21
Derrida, Jacques
   fragments   127
   otherness   137
   symbolic exchange   49–50
desert
   arid place   120–1
   environmental challenge   120
   inner silence of the body,
      extension of   122
   journey   123

natural and cultural of the
hyperreal 121–2
radical absence 122
site of something lost 121
wisdom 120
Disneyland 31

economic transactional
exchange 42
eschatology
America 81–2
Biblical narrative 81
heresy of impatience 86
singularity
event strike 91
kairòs 92–3
symbolic exchange 91–2
society without finality 84–5
terrorism
impossible exchange 89
Mauss' view 88–90
Platonic doctrine of
immortality of the
soul 87
seductive suicide 87
suicide-bombings 90
World Trade Centre
attack 89
time narratives
reversal process 83–4
slowing down process 82–3
temporal acceleration 82
Eucharistic Prayer
gift and reception 72
redeeming sacrifice 72
return-gift 72–3
evil
Biblical tradition 99
definition 96
and good
Bush, George W. 98
Manichaeism 99–100
power 99
principle 98

radical foreignness 97
virus 97
exchange
death of God 42, 46
economic transactional
exchange 42
exchange for capital 41–2
market exchange 42
object-exchange 48
exchange-value and use-
value 22–3

Fatal Strategies
ceremony 73–4
sacrament 79
subject and object 43
Feuerbach, Ludwig
*The Essence of
Christianity* 38–9,
151n. 52
Fiddes, Paul 130
*For a Critique of the Political
Economy of the Sign*
sexual difference 111–12
sign and symbol 69
symbolic exchange 47
use-value 21–2
Foucault, Michel
biopower 27
theory of resemblances 75
fragments
aphorism 125
Cool Memories 123
desert 126
poetic *see* poetic resolution
quasi-sacramental view 126–7
French influences 17

Galbraith, John K. 101
Gane, Mike
anthropology 14
poetic fragments 131
German influences 17–18
gift-exchange 47

good
  definition 95
  and globalization
    Christianity 104
    Church's contribution 105
    ecclesiology 104
    economic growth 101–2
    human dignity 102–3
    universality of values 103
Greer, Germain
  The Whole Woman 111,
    163n. 19

Hegel, Georg Wilhelm
    Friedrich 43, 152n. 10
  Marxism 17, 81
  *The Phenomenology of
    Mind* 113
  simulation 31
human body
  barring and
    segmenting 109–11
  beauty and eroticism 108
  gender and seduction *see*
    seduction
  reality television 108–9
  sacraments *see* sacramental
    body
  transsexual
    artificiality of gender
      identity 113–14
    Church 114–15
hyperreality
  fatal 49
  generalized exchange 42

ideas and meaning 12
Impossible Exchange
  atheism 56
  Mauss' logic of symbolic gift
    exchange 57–8
  nothing 140
  ruse of God 57
  virtual reality 58

integral reality 46
*In the Shadow of the Silent
    Majorities*
  idea of implosion 36
  rejection of sociology 36
  Western masses 35
Isaiah, Prophet 98–9

Jaulin, Robert
  La Mort Sara 49

kairòs
  connection 92
  Letter to the Ephesians 93
Kellner, Douglas 4, 150n. 25,
    154n. 45
  political criticims 31
  political criticisms 24
Kristeva, Julia
  language 15–16
  poetic fragments 131

Lacan, Jacques
  barred subject 110
  Symbolic Order 47
  unconscious 15
language 12–13
Lefebvre, Henri
  Critique of Everyday Life 17
  Notes Written One Sunday 68

Manichaeism 99–100
Marcuse, Herbert
  operationalism 69
  simulation 26–7
Marion, Jean-Luc
  The Blind at Shiloh 77
  God 130
  otherness 143
  sacramental singularities 77–8
Marxism
  Baudrillard rejection 24
  capitalist economy 18

mass media   29
The Matrix   4
Mauss, Marcel
    *The Gift: The Form and Reason
        for Exchange in Archaic
        Societies*
    death of God   57–8
    Eucharistic Prayer   72
    obligatory generosity   71
    otherness   137
    potlatch   154n. 37
    symbolic exchange   47, 50
    symbols   70
    violent death   88
McLuhan, Marshall
    the medium is the message
        29, 119
metaphysics of the code
    binary system   32–3
    digitality   33
    electoral participation
        34–5
    political and social
        participation   33–4
    *In the Shadow of the Silent
        Majorities*   35–6
Metz, Johann B.   39

Negri, Antonio
    evil   103–4
    kairòs   92–3
Nietzsche, Friedrich   168n. 41
    The Anti-christ   141
    aphorism   125
    death of God   2, 42, 57
    madman   95
nihilism   139
    John of the Cross   141
    Nietzsche's characterization of
        Christianity   141
non-event
    sacramental singularity   77
    violence   60–1
    war   59–60

Novak, Michael
    *The Spirit of Democratic
        Capitalism*   101
Nussbaum, Martha   101

object exchange
    festival and ritual   48
    genealogy of death   48–9
otherness
    absolute alterity   137–8
    autonomous selfhood   136
    communion   138
    connectedness   137–8
    mystical path   138
    recentring   139

Pawlett, William
    barred body   111
    impossible exchange   58
    sex   117
    The Perfect Crime   133
Platonic doctrine of immortality of
        the soul   87
poetic resolution   127
    Book of Proverbs   130
    Judeo-Christian theological
        perspective   129–30
    linguistic signification   129
    negation   129
    revelation   130
    trompe l'oeil   128
political and social
        participation   33
political economy *see* capitalist
        economy
Poster, Mark   109
postmodernity
    God   55–6
    hyperreality   42, 55
    post-structuralism   12
    potlatch   47
    precession of simulacra   17, 26,
        127
    fable of the devil   61–2

primitive societies
  concept of death 49
  death 80
  gift-exchange 47
  vs modern societies 14
psychology
  Freudian approach 15
  Kristeva's transfinite and
    symbolic 16

Radcliffe, Timothy 117
radical thought
  banal thinking 134
  The Perfect Crime 133–4
  prayer 135
  reasoned theorizing 134–5
  self-revealing object 133
redemption 95
Ricoeur, Paul 158n. 47
  poetry fragments 131
  sign and symbol 70
ruse of God 57

sacramental body
  baptism and Eucharist 115–16
  masculinity and
    femininity 116–17
  natural law 115
  seduction and law 118
  semiotic barring, resistant
    to 115–16
  sexuality 117
sacramentality
  Chauvet's symbols
    characteristics 71
    Eucharistic Prayer 72–3
    graciousness and
      gratuitousness 71–2
  sign and symbol
    Chauvet's view 70–3
    housing 69
    Paul Avis 70
    Paul Ricoeur's work 70
    wedding ring 69

singularity
  Marion's view 77–8
  nihilism 78–9
Saussure, Ferdinand
  12–13
Sebeok, Thomas 33
seduction
  codified society 53
  human body
    annul power relations 113
    feminist liberation 112
  play of appearances and
    form 52
  process of masking 52
  psychoanalysis 51
  sacramental body 118
self-revealing object 133
semiology 13
Shield, David, *Reality
    Hunger* 124–5
sign exchange-value *see*
    exchange-value
signs
  barring body 110
  Chauvet's view 70
  commodity 20, 29
  consumer society 20–1
  exchange-value 23
  language system 12–13
  meaning 13
  political and social
    participation 33
  political ideology 16
  religious affiliation 39
  unconscious 15
Simulacra and Simulation 27
simulacral religious community 39
simulation
  consumer capitalism 27
  hyperreal 29
    Disneyland 31
    metaphysics of the code *see*
      metaphysics of the code
    sign fetishism 31–2

signifiers 30
social salvation by
consumption 30–1
implosion of religion
Christianity 38–9
dangers, religious
practice 39–40
God 37–8
order of simulacra
production 29
Renaissance and
counterfeit 28–9
socio-political realm 33
symbolic exchange,
reality 29
situationalism 21
social critique 16, 43
evil 96
society without finality 84–5
Symbolic 15
symbolic exchange
affluence 60
beauty 109
Eucharistic Prayer, redeeming
sacrifice 72–3
gift-exchange 47
Mauss' ethnographic
analysis 50
otherness 136
seduction 112
codified society 53
play of appearances and
form 52
process of masking 52
psychoanalysis 51
singularity and
eschatology 91–2
taxation 45
waste 43–4
Symbolic Exchange and Death
ceremony 73–4
nihilism 140–1
order of simulacra 27
poetic fragments 128

seduction 53
sign and symbol 69
symbolic exchange 47–8
unconscious 15
symbols 48, 68–73, 78
The System of Objects 17,
20–1, 43

taxation 45
terrorism
impossible exchange 89
Mauss' view 88–90
Platonic doctrine of immortality
of the soul 87
seductive suicide 87
suicide-bombings 90
World Trade Centre attack 89
theological hyperreality 141–4
Tracy, David
fragments 126–7
The Transparency of Evil 96
Turner, Denys 138–9

unconscious 15
Underhill, Evelyn
radical otherness 138
use-value
exchange-value 22–3
people's needs 22

Vattimo, Gianni
nihilism 140
tabula rasa 139
The Violence of the Global 102

Ward, Graham
sacramental body 115–16
waste 43–4
Williams, Rowan 58

Žižek, Slavoj
global capitalism 153n. 18
simulacral religious practice 39
virtual war 60